Barrie Mahoney worked as a teacher and head teacher in the south west of England, and then became a school inspector in England and Wales. A new life and career as a newspaper reporter in Spain's Costa Blanca led to him launching and editing an English language newspaper in the Canary Islands. Barrie's books include novels in 'The Prior's Hill Chronicles' series, as well as books for expats in the 'Letters from the Atlantic' series, which give an amusing and reflective view of life abroad.

Barrie writes regular columns for newspapers and magazines in Spain, Portugal, Ireland, Australia, South Africa, Canada, UK and the USA. He also designs mobile apps and websites to promote the Canary Islands and expat life, and is often asked to contribute to radio programmes about expat life.

Visit the author's websites:

www.barriemahoney.com
www.thecanaryislander.com

Other books by Barrie Mahoney

Journeys & Jigsaws (The Canary Islander Publishing) 2013
ISBN: 978 184386 646 6 (Paperback and Kindle)

Threads and Threats (The Canary Islander Publishing) 2013
ISBN: 978 184386 645 9 (Paperback and Kindle)

Letters from the Atlantic (The Canary Islander Publishing) 2013
ISBN: 978-0992767136 (Paperback and Kindle)

Living the Dream (The Canary Islander Publishing) 2015
ISBN: 978-0992767198 (Paperback and Kindle)

Message in a Bottle (The Canary Islander Publishing) 2012 ISBN: 978-1480031005 (Paperback and Kindle)

Escape to the Sun (The Canary Islander Publishing) 2013
ISBN: 978-0957544444 (Paperback and Kindle)

Expat Voice (The Canary Islander Publishing) 2014
ISBN: 978-0992767174 (Paperback and Kindle)

Island in the Sun (The Canary Islander Publishing) 2015
ISBN: 978-0992767181 (Paperback and Kindle)

Expat Survival

Barrie Mahoney

The Canary Islander Publishing

© Copyright 2015

Barrie Mahoney

The right of Barrie Mahoney to be identified as author of this work has been asserted by him in accordance with the Copyright, Designs and Patents Act 1988.

All Rights Reserved

No reproduction, copy or transmission of this publication may be made without written permission. No paragraph of this publication may be reproduced, copied or transmitted save with the written permission of the author, or in accordance with the provisions of the Copyright Act 1956 (as amended).
Any person who commits any unauthorised act in relation to this publication may be liable to criminal prosecution and civil claims for damages.
A CIP catalogue record for this title is available from the British Library.

ISBN 978-0992767167
www.barriemahoney.com

First Published in 2012
Second Edition 2015

The Canary Islander Publishing

Acknowledgements

I would like to thank all those people that I have met on my journey to where I am now.

To supportive friends who helped me to overcome the many problems and frustrations that I faced and taught me much about learning to adapt to a new culture. Also, to friends in the UK, or scattered around the world, who have kept in touch despite being so far away.

To the people that I met whilst working as a newspaper reporter and editor in Spain and the Canary Islands, and for the privilege of sharing their successes and challenges in life.

To my nephew, Damon Mahoney, for his creative ideas and inspiration for the design of the cover of this book.

Disclaimer

This is a book about real people, real places and real events, but names of people and companies have been changed to avoid any embarrassment.

DEDICATION

In loving memory of my brother, Baden, and his wife, Sue

Contents	10
Preface	13
It Began with a Dream	14
Celebration	19
Canary Islands' Day	20
"Your hat looks wonderful, my dear"	22
The Twelve Grapes	26
The South American Factor	28
"It makes me feel alive"	32
"It's hot up my barranco!"	35
Culture and Heritage	38
Agatha Christie and the Canary Islands	39
The Whistle Language	42
"Is anyone here called Juan?"	45
An Explosive Island	48
Gadgets and Gizmos	51
Technology for Expats – Voip phones	52
Rediscovering Radio	55
Expats and Ebooks	58
Expat Television	61
Go Virtual	64
A Connection at the Mortuary	67
Food and Drink	70
The Vegetarian Expat	71
Fit to Drink?	75
Just a Trifle	78

A Mince Pie for Christmas	80
Baking Bread	83
Fancy a Cup of Coffee?	86
Marmite and Mosquitoes	89
Political	92
Voting in Spain	93
Flamenco – the Latest Weapon!	96
Getting into Hot Water	98
The European Family	101
Fluffy Tales	105
A Kitten in the Canaries	106
Vets and Pets	109
Vets at Home	112
How to Do It	115
Debit Cards for Expats	116
Complaining in Spain	119
Paternity Leave	122
"What's Your Address?"	125
Learning the Language	128
"You need new track rod ends, Sir"	132
Complaining	136
"I just wanna be OK, be OK, be OK…	137
A Tortoise called Aduana	141
How big is your gnome?	144
The Sunshine Expat	147
Expat Life	150
Beware of Submarines and Drug Smuggling Grannies	151

Weather Influences Walking	153
Mowing the Lawn	156
The Lollipop People	159
Collapse of the Euro?	162
"Maybe I want to go home?"	166
No Doors or Windows	167
Lightning Strike	170
Too Much of a Good Thing	173
Hypertension in the Canary Islands	176
Embalming anyone?	179
Expats and Recession	182
The Seven Year Itch	185
The beginning of the end, or is it the end of the beginning?	189

Preface

It began with a dream…

Since the publication of my earlier books, 'Letters from the Atlantic' and 'Living the Dream', I have received a number of emails and letters from would-be expats asking me to write some kind of 'How to do it' guide to living abroad. Suggestions made to me were along the lines of giving detailed instructions to would-be expats about taking those first tentative steps to a new life in another country.

At first, it seemed a good idea, but I quickly realised that my life in Spain and the Canary Islands has, and continues to have, many different challenges to those that the newly-arrived expat may face in Thailand, Canada or, indeed, France.

Legal issues, customs and traditions are very different in most countries, with even individual regions offering strange twists, turns and variations to national laws; the Canary Islands, as an autonomous province within Spain, is a good example of such individuality.

No, it seemed that there would have to be a very different approach to the one that was initially expected from me. I decided, therefore, to focus upon the expat - that confused being of mixed nationhood striving to find a place in a world of different cultures, traditions and often languages.

As a Brit, living abroad, I will always see the world through the eyes of a Brit, as I know that my Canarian neighbours see their world through the eyes of a Canarian, the Germans through the eyes of a German and so on. This sense of nationhood is within our very being and is very hard to ignore, regardless of how long we may live in our adopted countries.

The expression that "You can take the Brit out of Britain, but you will never take Britain out of the Brit" is a truism that I often quote, and remains true regardless of nationality.

Life for an expat usually begins with a dream; a dream that grows stronger each time we dream it, and is supported by prods and pokes in our daily lives.

I know from talking to many expats over the years that it starts with a feeling of restlessness that cannot be explained; it is a feeling that you should be somewhere else, and that you are missing something essential to your very being. Over time, the feeling grows until, rather like toothache, you just have to do something about it.

For me, like so many, it has something to do with culture, climate and lifestyle. As much as I loved, and still love the UK, I felt stifled and trapped by the culture that surrounded me. Of course, like so many, I found the winter months to be cruel; I missed the sunshine and being outdoors.

The final realisation came to me when I finally realised, as a school inspector working in all parts of England and Wales, that I only saw my Dorset home during daylight for about ten hours each week during the winter months. That was if I was lucky, because those precious daylight hours were often incarcerated in rain, snow or fog; winter months that seemed to go on forever.

I fell in love with Spain during one of my first overseas holidays, and this was to be the seed for the nagging pain of discontent that I felt for several years until my partner, David, and I finally did something about it. Even so, this book is not just about Spain, or the Canary Islands.

It is about a would-be expat wanting to escape to a life in the sun, and being faced with issues that require an attitude of survival. I talk about 'survival' in the loosest sense, as I am not talking about life and death situations, but situations that require a different view of life to be applied and relate to most expats everywhere.

Many expats that I know take their Britishness, Frenchness or Italianness too far. Many are unwilling to adjust to changing circumstances in their new lives. Many head towards national enclaves, which they regard as somehow 'safer', but miss out on the whole point of what it is to be an expat.

Some expats cannot be bothered to even attempt to learn the language, and develop a cynical indifference to local culture and traditions. Sadly, some expats also fall into the trap of being what I call 'The Sunshine Expat', who is basically only interested in the sunshine. He (or she, for that matter) tends to view life through a glass of cheap gin and tonic, and spends his days complaining about life in the UK, as well as in his newly adopted country.

"It was never like this in Huddersfield (substitute this for any town in the UK)", is often a grumble to be heard on 'The Sunshine Expat's' balcony. At the first sign of trouble, 'The Sunshine Expat' heads back to his country of birth, with his tail between his legs.

The true expat feels a genuine sense of being in the right place and not just where he happens to be, based upon an accident of birth. Each day is an adventure, a new chapter to be read, a lifestyle to be tasted and savoured. The true expat also quickly realises that it is not about what he can get from his adopted country, but also what he can give back in return. This book is based upon my weekly 'Letters from the Atlantic' that are published in a number of magazines and newspapers across the world.

Each 'Letter' is intended to be a light-hearted account and a reflection of my own life as an expat over a period of one year. Some may make readers laugh, whilst others may make readers cry in despair or even anger, yet others are meant to be a gentle prod in what I have found to be the right direction for me.

Please do not think that I always get it right either, I don't, and feel the same sense of failure and frustration in common with most expats everywhere. This is not a 'Do it yourself guide' either, but a few thoughts on the best way to survive in a country that is your choice and not merely an accident of birth.

Celebration

Canary Islands' Day (Día de las Canarias)

30 May is a day for all Canarians, as well as for all those who love the Canary Islands, to be proud! Proud of our beautiful islands, our rich heritage, the way of life and the enjoyment that they give to so many people. This is the day when the Canary Islands, a Spanish Autonomous Community, became integrated into the European Union as a peripheral territory deserving of preferential treatment. It marks the anniversary of the autonomous Canary Islands' Parliament's first session, which took place on May 30, 1983.

The Canary Islands are a long way away from the Spanish Peninsular, yet are very much part of Spain and also part of Europe. It is easy to forget that Gran Canaria is at the southernmost tip of Europe and our closest neighbours are those parts of Africa with a more European outlook.

The islands are a bridge between Africa and Europe with a strong link to parts of America. It is worth remembering that America opened its doors wide for the thousands of Canary Islanders who crossed the Atlantic in times of hardship looking for a better future. Many have since returned with their children and grandchildren. Europeans, Africans, Asians and Americans meet in the Canary Islands, a true intercultural link and an open, welcoming land for the millions of tourists who come to discover the beauty of these islands.

Many cultural activities and celebrations are arranged for Canary Islands' Day each year. Schools make a special point of teaching children about the rich history and culture of the Canary Islands and organise parties and events for children in the days before the special day. Many people hold private parties at home or in restaurants on the evening of May 29. It is a time for great celebration and joy.

Now for the history and geography lessons. The Canary Islands consist of seven inhabited islands off the coast of Africa, which are: Gran Canaria, Fuerteventura, Lanzarote, Tenerife, El Hierro, La Palma and La Gomera.

There is also the Chinijo Archipelago, which includes the tiny islands of La Graciosa, Alegranza, Montaña Clara, Roque del Este and Roque del Oeste. Although these islands form an autonomous community within Spain, they are closer to Morocco and the Western Sahara. The Romans too were aware of the Canary Islands, but they remained independent until the Spanish invasion of the islands in 1402, when the islands became part of the Kingdom of Castile in 1495.

This is a day when we celebrate with pride and wish to share just a taste of these wonderful islands with our visitors, as well as those who live and work here. If you have never visited us, maybe one day you should.

"Your hat looks wonderful, my dear!"

Nothing says "Royal Wedding" quite like an ostrich's bottom joined to your left temple. No, I had told myself, I would not be spending the day watching the wedding celebrations and associated hats of a couple I did not know, would never meet and who were representing a country many miles away. It was a country that I had left many years ago and would be unlikely to return to.

Participating in such an event from a small island in the Atlantic did seem a ridiculous way to spend a day, when I had far better things to do. Although I respect and admire the Queen, I suspect that is more to do with the fact that she represents continuity in my life, rather than a wish to celebrate the wedding of her grandson. I had another chapter of my book to write, and that was the way that I fully intended to spend the Royal Wedding Day.

How wrong I was. After being initially drawn by the excitement that was building on the radio, curiosity led me to switch on the television. The atmosphere was infectious, and by 10.00am, I found myself watching and sharing the events on television with around 2 billion other people in at least 150 countries around the world.

The enthusiasm and excitement of the crowds waiting and watching brushed away all the usual cares and sorrows of the world. Gone, for the day anyway, were thoughts of war, rebellion, recession, bankers' bonuses and students' tuition fees.

In its place came a kind of raw innocence, one of belief and hope for the future, and a sense that history was being made without the intervention and manipulations of politicians and big business. It was a simple hope and belief in the future that the union of two people always brings, and an infectious joy that is so hard to put into words.

How we marvelled at the hats - as ridiculous as some of them were. After all, wearing a dead parrot, or the entire contents of a florist's catalogue on your head does not look particularly 'cool', or stylish come to that. "Please do not turn your head whilst in the pew, Madam, otherwise you will flatten the gentleman to your left."

Did these ladies actually look at themselves in the mirror before they left home? Were their partners too frightened to make a negative comment, or were they just too subdued after being crammed into a morning suit and trussed up like chickens for the day?

I suspect that one of the young princesses, who was wearing part of a tree on her head, learned the hard way when the cameras caught her leaning forward at an angle of 90° in order for the limousine to accommodate both her and her generously proportioned hat on the way to the palace for the obligatory canapés!

Spirits were lifted whilst listening to the music of some of the great British composers in the spectacular and familiar surroundings of Westminster Abbey, now decked with beautiful, fresh green trees.

Innocent looking and freshly scrubbed choirboys singing their new M & S socks off, fusty Archbishops, Cardinals and Deans, with far too much white facial hair, all brought back memories of earlier times of national celebrations long ago.

Along with most other people watching, I was drawn into the spirit of an event that I could not explain. Watching the beautiful bride and her handsome prince is, I guess, the stuff of fairy tales and early childhood memories.

Yes, I too felt a lump rising in my throat and found that I had moist eyes at several times during the service. This was surreal and quite ridiculous to be feeling and behaving like this, I told myself.

Mums, dads, children, grannies and granddads swarmed down the Mall to watch the newly wedded couple appear on the balcony. A sea of different coloured skins, ages and nationalities greeted the cameras.

Awkward and surly looking teenagers admitting that they too were having a great time and were waiting to see 'that kiss' made me feel that I had somehow slipped into an alternative universe for the day, but maybe that was the effect of Victoria Beckham's spiky alien creation. People were just so happy!

Later I found myself attending a 'Royal' barbecue and joining in with a toast to the happy couple. It was a sincere toast, not only to the Royal couple, but to the love of all couples everywhere, gay or straight, and with the sincere hope that they will have found their soul-mates and can live in happiness together for many years to come.

The Twelve Grapes

Tradition has it that on New Year's Eve in Spain and the Canary Islands, twelve 'lucky grapes' known as 'Uvas de la Suerte' have to be eaten around the stroke of midnight. It is important to eat one grape at a time with each stroke of the clock and, of course, washed down with liquid refreshment, and usually a lively Spanish bubbly wine called Cava.

It is believed that this tradition came from ancient wine growers; well, after all it does fuel the sale of grapes on New Year's Eve doesn't it?

This fine tradition, as with a number of so-called traditions, has a number of flaws. Without appearing too cynical about the whole business of grape swallowing, I have witnessed several unfortunate incidents concerning the hasty swallowing of grapes since I have lived in Spain, and I repeat these as a warning for this and future New Year's celebrations.

Most importantly, grapes grown in the Canary Islands are of the seeded variety. The process of hastily swallowing twelve grapes in twelve seconds may be perfectly acceptable with the unseeded variety, but what exactly do you do with the pips in the seeded type when you are in polite company and do not wish to swallow them?

My Mum used to warn me about swallowing grape seeds with the threat that I may get an immediate attack of appendicitis and would have to be whisked to the casualty department of the nearest hospital for an immediate operation.

It is strange how memories from childhood are triggered by small events in later life. According to Mum, this pip swallowing may lead to an acute case of peritonitis and if you were really unlucky you would be dead before the end of New Year's Day. Yes, Mum was a little inclined to exaggeration when it came to matters medical. All that inconvenience for a grape pip. Is it really worth all the trouble?

I recall one unfortunate occasion at a New Year's party that I attended in the Costa Blanca, when an elderly lady swallowed a pip that 'went down the wrong way'. It started as a cough, gentle at first and then becoming increasing violent. She was given a glass of wine and later a glass of water to ease the problem.

Her coughing became increasing troublesome and I really did not like the shade of pink that she was turning, as a few helpful people thumped her vigorously on the back to dislodge the offending item. Sadly it was to no avail until one helpful gentleman, who claimed to be a first aider, wrapped his arms around her chest from behind and gave her a sudden squeeze. The old lady moaned, and not with pleasure, as her false teeth shot across the room. The offending pip had been dislodged and the party continued with the old lady later leading the Hokey Cokey.

So have a wonderful New Year and remember the old adage, 'It is always safer to spit than swallow.'

The South American Factor

The Canary Islands have a richness, colour and diversity that are probably unequalled in most parts of Europe. No, I am not talking about the flora and fauna of these islands, but its people. Here you will find people of all colour, faith and no faith, straight, gay and transgendered. In the main, all rub along happily with each other and this is one of the many reasons why I adore these islands so much.

The islands offer a culture of 'live and let live' with tremendous energy, vitality and enthusiasm - feelings and impressions that are quickly sensed by our many thousands of tourists to the islands and why they return year after year.

One of my favourite events in Gran Canaria is Carnival in Las Palmas and I would urge anyone who has not experienced this colourful and amazing spectacular to choose (or make) a costume, pack a bag and stay in Las Palmas for a couple of nights during the height of the festival.

Be prepared to stay up all night and be hoarse by the end of it all! If you hate late nights, loud noise, crowds of people and thoroughly enjoying yourself then please don't go! So why is it that Carnival is larger and livelier than most events that you will find anywhere in Europe? I put it down to the South American factor.

My dentist, accountant, lawyer and eye surgeon are all from Argentina, and very good they are too. As most residents will already have discovered, there are many people from South America living and working in these islands and this is one of the reasons why Carnival in Las Palmas is sometimes described as "Second only to Rio".

It certainly puts Peninsular Spain to shame when it comes to this spectacular annual event. Indeed, many professional people, as well as bar and restaurant staff from South America, now live and work in the Canary Islands. It is interesting to talk to some of these people and to discover the reasons why they are attracted to these small islands in the Atlantic.

Since the 18th century there has been an outflow of Canary Islanders to parts of South America and to parts of what is now the USA. At one time this was part of Spain's strategy to colonise and populate the newly discovered Americas, and the Spanish Government looked to the Canary Islands for recruits to increase the size of the army in Louisiana, with the dual role of defending the territory, as well as populating it.

In more recent times, there was an outflow of migrants from Spain and the Canary Islands and particularly during the periods of economic troubles, avoidance of the obligatory military service, the 1936 - 1939 Civil War, as well as during the period of General Franco's dictatorship between 1939 and 1975.

During this time, many Spanish citizens fled from Spain as a result of the Civil War, as well as sending their children to South America for protection. These refugees from Spain eventually settled in Argentina, Cuba and Mexico, as well as other countries in Latin America.

Cuba was a particularly welcoming destination for many Canarians and there are still strong links between the Canary Islands and Cuba, at both the Islands' Government and personal levels. There remains a strong feeling of gratitude towards this island in the Caribbean that became home to so many Canarians fleeing from repression and poverty.

Many of these migrants are now of an age when they wish to return to their country of birth and Spain, to its credit, is doing its best to help these Spanish emigrants and particularly by supporting the elderly. Pensions, as well as return visits to Spain for these 'children of the Civil War' and who have not visited their country of origin for many years are now provided by the Spanish Government in an attempt to redress some of the injustices that forced them into exile during the Franco dictatorship.

Temporary changes to Spanish law under the 'Law of Historical Memory' has allowed many children and grandchildren of Spanish emigrants living in Latin American to obtain Spanish citizenship.

At times of financial crisis, history teaches us that the weakest and most vulnerable members of society are often singled out for criticism and often worse.

We heard a great deal about the perceived problems of immigration into the UK during the last General Election. However, in the Canary Islands, we can reflect upon this as a more positive story and one that has contributed greatly to island life.

It makes me feel alive!

Expats tend to spend a great deal of time at airports. My regular visits to the airport often give me the opportunity to indulge in one of my favourite past times - people watching. Although I tend to avoid the misery of 'Departures' like the plague, watching the 'Arrivals' is always an entertaining business. 'Spot where they are from' - is quite an easy game for me to play nowadays, and one that I rather enjoy.

I can easily spot an Irishman, a German or a Spanish national with just a quick glance, although defining which Scandinavian country the tourist is from does require a much more detailed observation. It is amazing how comedy stereotypes of the individual characteristics of different nationalities are often so true. As for spotting an Englishman, well that is just so easy, although I sometimes do get them confused with Germans – yes, the two nationalities really are alike in so many ways!

My eye was drawn to a young man in a wheelchair being pushed by an elderly woman from the arrivals lounge and into the main airport corridor. He looked painfully thin, with a pallid unhealthy looking skin, and his frail body was strapped into his wheelchair.

An elderly man followed the wheelchair, pushing several suitcases on one of the airport trolleys. It was clear that these passengers did not travel light. I immediately recognised the Welsh accent as being from the valleys when the elderly woman began speaking to the young man.

However, I could not decide whether the elderly couple accompanying the young man were his elderly parents or grandparents.

The young man beamed as soon as he was pushed into the corridor. "Look Ma! Look!" he shouted, "The sun! The sun's shining on our island again!" The old lady nodded, "Yes, Colin, it is. You like it here don't you?" She took a tissue out of her pocket and wiped the young man's mouth gently.

Colin caught my eye. I smiled. He beamed at me, displaying a broad, toothy smile. It was a genuine smile, full of happiness and joy.

"Hello," I said. "You look really pleased to be here. I hope you had a good flight?"

Colin nodded, and beamed again. "I love it here. I always love it here. It makes me feel alive".

I smiled and nodded, and wished the young man a happy holiday and moved on to my next errand.

Later, whilst waiting at the Post Office, I began to think about Colin and his elderly parents. His words, "It makes me feel alive" played on my mind. Colin was clearly disabled physically, as well as mentally.

He looked so poorly, yet I have rarely seen a smile so broad and genuine, a smile of pure elation and joy, as I did on this young man.

As I was leaving the airport, I spotted Colin's father waiting for a taxi. I suspected that they were waiting for one especially designed for disabled visitors. "Colin's going to have a really good time," I said. "I can see it in his face."

The old man nodded. "Yes, we try to come here as much as we can. He loves the island and is so much better when he is here. We don't know how much longer Colin will be with us, but we want to make sure that each day is special for him. He gives us so much joy".

I left the airport with a lump in my throat, reflecting about this very special young man and his caring, loving parents. I hope the family have a truly wonderful holiday and that Colin can store many happy memories for the future.

Happiness and joy is contained within us and is a state of mind. It need not be connected to our health, mental and physical abilities, the amount of money that we have or the amount of booze that we consume. I think I am beginning to understand what Colin meant when he said, "It makes me feel alive."

"It's Hot Up My Barranco!"

"Phew, it's hot up my barranco today, darling," gasped Miranda as she staggered down the street carrying two large and heavy bags of clattering bottles from the local supermarket. Before you get too carried away by imagining a doctor about to don a pair of surgical gloves for some emergency female probing, I should explain that Miranda is one of the village's more colourful characters.

She is a school assistant in one of the less classy private schools by day and a tattooist by night. I once asked if there was any conflict of interest between her two jobs. She screeched loudly in my ear, before resting her mug of gin on top of my car.

"No, not at all, darling. It's a great way to help the kids with their reading."

I must have looked puzzled, as I thought I knew a thing or two about teaching children to read, and she seemed to read my thoughts.

"You see, I have all the letters of the alphabet tattooed all over my body somewhere, so I use those to help children to read. If it's Tina the Tiresome Transvestite we are reading, I just point out this letter "T" on my arm and then we find the picture of the Tina on my back. Easy, the kids love it."

"So you have all the letters and associated pictures somewhere on your body?"

"Oh, yes, darling, but I should say that some are more difficult to find than others. We tend to keep off the "Y" and "Z" words otherwise I would get the sack, darling. If you know what I mean!" She guffawed loudly, as she nudged me in the ribs and winked knowingly.

By now, I think you are probably getting the idea of what Miranda is like. A lovely lady, but back in the UK I would be surprised if she had a job at all. However, over here, we are all much more open-minded.

As Miranda dropped her bags by my front gate and she propped herself on my parked car, she watched what I was doing with some amusement. I stopped washing the hedge (actually it is one of those plastic ones, but I do like to freshen it up a bit from time to time) and it is always a good opportunity to remove the crisp packets and condoms from its branches.

"You are home early today. Is everything alright?"

"Darling, it's the heat. It is just so hot. I tell you, darling, it was 41°C up my barranco at lunchtime. It was just too much darling. We sent the little dears home early, because they were just fading away."

I tried to imagine Miranda's boisterous pupils fading away and thought it highly unlikely. We have a number of calimas, although some people call them siroccos, on the islands each year, and the islanders are generally conditioned to withstand them, and it is the expats who suffer.

They can be a little unpleasant for a few days, bringing with them very high temperatures from Africa and the Sahara.

In my own village, when the wind disappears, it is a case of staying inside as much as possible with air-conditioning on and plenty of cool drinks. These heat waves can occur at any time during the year, but they are less common during the cooler months.

Miranda's school is situated in a barranco, a Spanish word for ravine. Some would say that was a foolish place to build anything, because of potential sudden rainstorms, but I guess the land was cheap. Anyway, I suspect it was built to withstand the heat and would have air conditioning installed as essential.

"I was pleased to get home early, darling. I needed to get ready for the bonfire this evening."

"Bonfire? In this heat!" I exclaimed.

"Darling, tomorrow is the Festival of St John the Baptist. A most important religious festival! You mustn't miss that. We are having a bonfire party tonight to celebrate. Not here you understand, but outside Telde. It's traditional you know, darling. You really must come. You don't have to be a Catholic, just bring a bottle!"

So there we have it. We are in the middle of a calima where daytime temperatures are around 40°C, in the shade, and the good people of Telde are planning a bonfire party to celebrate St John the Baptist. The activities on this island never cease to surprise me.

Culture and Heritage

Agatha Christie and the Canary Islands

Many residents and holidaymakers are well aware of the recuperative properties of the Canary Islands, yet few know of the strong links between the popular novelist, Agatha Christie, and these islands.

Agatha Christie visited the Canary Islands in search of a tranquil and recuperative environment to help her calm a troubled mind. In February 1927, at the age of 36, she visited the Canary Islands to recover from a number of events that had taken place in her life and were having a serious impact upon her mental health.

She mysteriously disappeared for eleven days in a 'fugue state', a rare psychiatric disorder characterised by amnesia of identity, memories and personality. The state is usually short-lived - sometimes a few hours, but others may suffer for a few days or even longer.

When her first marriage failed, Agatha Christie disappeared from her home and stayed at the Swan Hydro Hotel in Harrogate, under the name of the woman with whom her husband was having an affair. A young journalist, who used some of the story patterns in her books to suggest her likely moves, finally found her.

Agatha Christie's mother had recently died after a serious illness, her husband was in love with another woman and Agatha was having serious financial difficulties.

Each of these problems, particularly when combined, could be a recipe for, what most of us would call, a mental breakdown. It is this series of events in her personal life that led Agatha Christie to the Canary Islands.

Agatha and her daughter, Rosalind, together with her secretary, Charlotte Fisher, arrived in Tenerife on 4 February 1927. They stayed at the Gran Hotel Taoro in Puerto de la Cruz, which was the best hotel in Tenerife and the centre of the British community.

It is believed that in Puerto de la Cruz, Agatha Christie completed one of her novels, 'The Mystery of the Blue Train', which sold well and put an end to her financial worries. There is now a bronze bust of Agatha Christie and a street named after her in Puerto de la Cruz.

Having completed her novel, she decided to stay one more week in the Canary Islands to relax. Agatha longed for white sandy beaches rather than a sloping volcanic beach, and on 27 February decided to leave Tenerife and complete the remainder of her holiday in Gran Canaria, before returning to England by steamship on 4 March 1927.

Agatha Christie stayed at the Metropole Hotel in Las Palmas de Gran Canaria, which is opposite the beautiful Santa Catalina beach. Agatha described Las Palmas as the ideal place to go in the winter.

Sadly, the Metropole Hotel is no more and is now part of Las Palmas Town Hall, and is where I recently paid my fine for illegal parking! The British Club and their tennis courts were nearby and Agatha Christie began to write 'The Companion', included in her collection of short stories, 'The Thirteen Problems', which has strong links to Gran Canaria.

The Canary Islands made a clear impression upon the mind of this prolific author, and feature in a number of her stories such as 'The Man from the Sea' in the book, 'The Mysterious Mr. Quin', which also takes place on an island.

Agatha Christie was a much-travelled woman who visited Europe, South Africa, Australia, North America and the Middle East. It is a compliment to the Canary Islands that it was in these islands that she found the peace and tranquillity that she was looking for. The last word, and recommendation, must go to Agatha Christie with an extract from 'The Companion':

"I had had a breakdown in health and was forced to give up my practice in England and go abroad. I practised in Las Palmas, which is the principal town of Gran Canaria. In many ways I enjoyed the life out there very much. The climate was mild and sunny, there was excellent surf bathing..."

So there we have it. If you are in need of a recuperative break, sun and relaxation, you know where to come!

The Whistle Language

I am often asked, "What are the most important things to do when planning to move to another country?" My answer is always the same, "Learn the language, and preferably before you arrive". I have learned Spanish the hard way and, because I do not find learning languages particularly easy, it has taken me considerable time and a determined effort to succeed.

I blame my early education. As an eleven-year-old growing up in rural Lincolnshire, I was forced to learn French and Latin. I did not mind Latin too much, even though I failed to see the relevance of learning a dead language. Yet, I was told that Latin was essential if I wanted to be a doctor or a pharmacist, but as I cannot stand the sight of blood that was going to be highly unlikely!

Still, I liked the teacher and it could be faintly amusing chanting "amo, amas, amant" and all the rest of this ancient nonsense from my fusty textbook.

It was learning French that I really detested. Whether it was the teacher, who always seemed to exude just a hint of garlic rather than after shave, the boring pre-war edition of the text book, or the fact that I would much rather have been doing something else, as the sound of the language did not sit easily upon my ears. I became a clock-watcher willing the lesson to end. I began to dread the lessons and gave up the subject at the earliest opportunity.

The experience very nearly put me off learning languages for life until I had a shot at Russian, but that is a story for another time...

There is a small and very beautiful Canary Island called La Gomera. The island has a population of around 22,000 people, and the islanders have maintained a very special way of communicating with each other. In early times, the aboriginal population, the Guanches, used a whistle language to convey complex messages across the deep valleys.

As a whistle can be heard from a long distance away, it was far more effective than shouting, and much faster than travelling across the rugged landscape.

When the Romans conquered the islands, they documented this language, which in Spanish is known as El Silbo Gomero, or simply El Silbo. In the 16th century, after the islands were colonised by Spanish settlers, this language was adapted to Spanish, and it still survives today.

Silbo Gomero is not a language in its own right, but it is a way of echoing syllables of words by putting fingers in the mouth, and can be heard over distances of around three thousand metres.

Pitch, intensity, length, and intermittent or continuous sounds are used to distinguish the different phonemes and syntax. I am told that the grammar and vocabulary of El Silbo Gomero are exactly the same as in Spanish. It is at the same time, both an eerie yet strangely wonderful sound to hear and experience.

Nowadays, with telephones, mobiles and broadband Internet calls, there is no longer a need to communicate by whistling. However, as we learned from the recent electrical storms on the islands, when many of us lost electricity, telephone and even mobile telephone connections, a back up alternative is always a good idea! Thanks to a local government initiative, El Silbo Gomero is taught at every school on the island to ensure that future generations will still remember and use it.

Learning Latin as an eleven-year-old? No, I still do not see the point. Even though I am told that a good grasp of Latin would make the learning of other languages easier, it did not work for me. Learning the Whistle Language? Now that is a different matter, and I wish that it had been on the curriculum when I was a confused eleven-year-old. I'm just off to practice!

Is anyone here called Juan?

I am very fond of pizza; that is if I can find one that is vegetarian. Being vegetarian, I have sometimes found it very difficult to get across the message that a 'pizza vegetal' is pizza without the inclusion of flesh of any kind. I have been presented with supposedly vegetarian pizzas laced with generous dollops of tuna, a fried egg and even a generous sprinkling of ham, which I thought was red pepper, before my stomach started heaving and I headed like a bullet for the door.

No, it has not been easy being a vegetarian in Spain and the Canary Islands, but I have now found the perfect pizzeria, or cafe bar to be more accurate. Personally, I think that the pizzas produced there are some of the best on the island - a perfect combination of a thin, not too crisp base and a perfectly cooked range of seasonal vegetables. We often have a take away pizza ready for a night in front of the television with a good film.

A few days ago I telephoned to place our usual order. Instead of the usually cheery bar owner/chef answering the telephone, came a sleepy voice. "Er, can you call back later please? The ovens have still not heated up".

I thought this strange, as the cafe bar opened at 7.00pm and by now it was nearly 8.00pm, which I know is still very early for Canarians to eat. I hoped that this was not the beginning of the end for yet another cafe bar, forced to lay off staff and eventually close because of the effects of the recession.

When I finally arrived at the bar to collect my order, the chef gave me a cheeky grin and told me that he was thankful for my call, because he had overslept and my call had woken him! The bar was, by now, full of elderly and middle aged men, some with a beer in hand watching sport on the television, others playing on the gaming machine, whilst others simply propped themselves against the bar, no drink in hand, but obviously there just for the company.

One younger man was cheerfully helping himself to a shot from behind the bar - after all, the bar owner was still cooking my pizzas, yet I noticed he carefully placed a number of coins by the till. It was a very Canarian scene.

Suddenly the door burst open and a small boy of about six or seven ran into the bar frantically waving a mobile phone above his head.

"Anyone in here called Juan?" he yelled (in Spanish, of course).

Suddenly the noise stopped, all the men turned and faced the small boy and three quarters of them stood up and shouted back "I'm Juan", before helpless laughter broke out in the bar.

The small boy looked puzzled before he ran off followed by several of the men. I would love to have known what the urgent message was about.

Although I have not checked any surveys of the most popular names used in the Canary Islands, I would guess, without a doubt, that the most popular name for men of a certain age in my village is Juan, and the best place to find them is in our pizzeria.

An Explosive Island

The Canary Islands have a history that is, quite literally, littered with explosions. Each of the seven main islands was created by hot volcanic lava pushing through the cold Atlantic Ocean in the last million years or so.

It therefore does not seem surprising that an occasional 'belch' can be heard, and seen, every few hundred years or so. One of our islands has been in a bit trouble over recent weeks, but first, a little background.

The Canary Islands are home to the third largest volcano in the world, Mount Teide, on the island of Tenerife, which is also the highest mountain in Spain. Interestingly, all the islands, except La Gomera, have seen volcanic activity in the last million years or so.

The island of El Hierro was formed over one million years ago. After three successive eruptions, the island emerged from the ocean as a triangle topped with a volcanic cone more than 2,000 metres high. Continued volcanic activity resulted in the island expanding to the island boasting the largest number of volcanoes in the Canary Islands, together with a multitude of caves and volcanic galleries.

Until recent weeks, most people had never even heard of El Hierro, also called the Meridian Island, which is the smallest and furthest south and west of the Canary Islands.

However, it is a fascinating place and rich in history, customs and traditions and one, which has, mercifully, escaped much of the ravages of the present day tourist industry.

It is the kind place that tourists should forget if interested only in copious quantities of booze, sunshine and discos when on holiday, because they will be greatly disappointed.

The stoic people of El Hierro are currently coping with the release of foul smelling gas, water stained by sulphur from the volcano and increased sea temperatures, which are killing fish and threatening all marine life in the area. Residents of the fishing village of La Restinga, which is the most affected area, were forced to leave their homes as the volcano just off the coast began erupting for the second time.

A string of earthquakes was registered on the island, including several tremors measuring above 4 on the Richter scale. However, in recent days villagers have been allowed to return to their homes, after scientists said they are not expecting an imminent eruption, although they admitted that the possibility of further after-shocks still exists.

Without making light of a potentially serious situation for the islanders of El Hierro, the volcanic cone that is currently pumping out magma 500 feet below the surface of the ocean is gradually heading towards the surface and experts tell us will shortly break the surface to create another Canary Island, in much the same way as these 'Fortunate Islands' were created millions of years ago.

Indeed, island residents are already brainstorming names for the potential landmass, including 'Discovery Island' and 'Atlantis', amongst other suggestions. Maybe, in years to come, future generations of tourists will be heading out to holiday on the newest baby of the Canary Islands.

El Hierro has lost much of the tourist income that is the lifeblood of this beautiful and unique island. Island residents estimate that the crisis has already cost them around 4 million euros in lost earnings from the Island's restaurants, hotels and diving schools. However, according to the locals, business had picked up in the last few days with increasing numbers of people curious to see the volcano, as its underwater eruption was visible from the air.

Curiously, it is the media who are hyping the story to an extent where inaccurate reports question the very survival of the island. This is nonsense, and many islanders simply describe it as "A little local difficulty" (in Spanish of course!). Indeed, as one of our island friends put it so eloquently the other day, "Without volcanoes there would not have been the Canary Islands". It is a fair point, I think.

Gadgets and Gizmos

Technology for Expats – VOIP Telephones

It is a fact of expat life that when we move overseas we spend much more time chatting on the telephone and our phone bills soar. The introduction of new telephone services such as Skype and Voip have recently made life so much easier, and cheaper, for the expat.

My Great Aunt Gertie hates phoning me in Spain. A long distance call from Manchester to Bournemouth is perfectly acceptable, even at peak rate; however, when it comes to a call from the UK to the Canary Islands, I hear the sharp inward sucking through her false teeth and a breathless "I must be quick, dear, I am calling long distance. It is very expensive, dear." My usual response of "No, Auntie you have this number on Friends and Family…" makes no difference.

Great Aunt Gertie also complains about, "That Spanish lady. I can't understand a word she's saying…"

"No Auntie, you won't, because you don't speak Spanish," is my forlorn defence of Telefonica's automated response that Auntie will sometimes hear if I am not in.

Mobile phone? I hear you say. Sadly not, as that causes an even worse problem for Auntie. "You'll have to speak up, dear. It is such a long way away."

I realised long ago that the telephone issue would have to be sorted if I was not to be banished from Auntie's will. I tried Skype, a wonderful service, but even though I bought Auntie a Skype phone, which didn't need a computer, thankfully, she still complained endlessly about the call quality.

Then I discovered part of the answer. She always insisted upon putting her false teeth in when using the Skype phone, which seemed to also affect her hearing. For some strange reason she claimed that she felt naked without them. Usually she didn't bother with false teeth, following a very unpleasant argument with her dentist and a small bottle of gin, yet she can still crack a nut like a teenager.

Why she had to put her teeth in when speaking on the Skype phone, I shall never know, but I suspect that it was because the magic box looked a little like a camera.

In despair, I turned to a wonderful new system called Voip (Voice over Internet Protocol). Without dealing too much with the technicalities, these clever telephones look and behave just like a normal telephone and can be easily used, as long as you have an Internet connection.

You don't need to have a computer switched on; indeed, you don't even need a computer. I have a cordless version, which means I can wander anywhere in the house or outside and still be connected.

Now this is the clever part. The Voip service that I use gave me a UK telephone number; actually, I bought one with a Bournemouth code, as I used to live there and I still have a lingering attachment to that fine seaside town. I now have a UK (Bournemouth) telephone number that Auntie Gertie and all my friends and family can dial at a local call rate, or free with some telephone packages.

The call is diverted to my Voip phone in the Canary Islands, and at no cost to me either. The call quality is excellent and even Auntie Gertie often comments that it sounds as if I am in the next room, and I am not shouting!

The other clever part about this system is that if I am out of the house, but in range of a Wifi or 3G mobile telephone signal, the call is diverted automatically to my iPhone free of charge as part of my mobile Internet package. I can be shopping in my local supermarket and still chat to Auntie Gertie, with or without teeth!

For me, having a UK phone number has proved to be invaluable as publishers, relatives and friends seem to be much happier calling me on my local UK number than calling my Spanish home number. I am not in the business of selling telephone services or equipment, but if you would like further information have a look at my website. Great Aunt Gertie is now quite happy with the arrangement and she assures me regularly that I am still mentioned in her will!

Rediscovering Radio

As much as many expats such as myself enjoy living in our newly adopted countries, it is strange what we miss from our countries of origin. Lemon Curd, Persil tablets and Branston pickle are just a few of the items that I know our friends beg visitors to bring when they visit.

For me, it is Marmite, mince pies and 'J' cloths that ensure that our visitors receive a particularly warm welcome. I also miss BBC radio news, as well as radio drama.

I have recently rediscovered radio, bringing with it memories of the illicit thrill of listening to pop radio stations under the bed covers late at night. The breath of fresh air that these radio stations brought to the airwaves gave a new energy for youngsters such as myself growing up during those grey, and often dismal times, in fenland Lincolnshire.

Later, it would be Radio 4 that I would listen to during my long car journey to school each day. This was something that I greatly missed when we moved to Spain and the Canary Islands.

Yes, I know that I can easily listen to any radio station in the world via the computer. However, sitting in front of a computer listening to radio does seem to be a very strange and uncomfortable activity and one that I soon dismissed as a complete waste of time.

After all, one of the joys of radio is that you can do something else at the same time, isn't it? How I missed listening to radio plays that seemed to create both colour and characterisation in my imagination in a way that film and television can never do.

Just before Christmas I ordered one of the new Internet radio receivers from the UK. They are not easy to get on the island and the Roberts radio that I wanted had particular features that were unique to the product. As long as I have a Wi-Fi Internet signal, or indeed a wired Internet connection, I can now listen to any radio station in the world. Radio 4, Classic FM, local radio from the Costa Blanca, as well as from my home town of Bournemouth are now regular features of my day.

How I enjoy listening to the gritty questioning when John Humphries challenges the Prime Minister about the latest budget cuts. Relaxing music and plays, as well as knowing that there are problems at the Cemetery Junction in Bournemouth yet again, as well as hearing what the Mayor of Torrevieja is up to in Spain, help me to maintain contact with places that I still love and have happy memories of.

In addition to all the thousands of radio stations that I can enjoy whatever I am doing in the house, there is also a new, very clever feature, called Last FM. This is a feature built into the radio whereby I can select my favourite genre of pop music and listen to this 'personal library' of music without the inane interruptions and burblings from would-be DJs and radio 'presenters'. It is pure bliss!

I hasten to add that I also listen to Canary Islands News as well as Spanish News, but I tend to pass on the rest. After all, there are only so many TV quiz shows and reality television programmes that any relatively sane person can take.

Expats and eBooks

I miss books! One of the most difficult things that I had to do when we left the UK for Spain was to cull my collection of books. We could neither afford to transport them all, nor was there going to be enough storage space in our new Spanish home to accommodate them. Book lovers will know the feeling, I am sure, that books become like old friends - always there to provide words of comfort and support in times of difficulty, laughter as well as endless sources of wisdom collected over the years.

In the end, I had to make a decision and most of my collection of books found their way to the Salvation Army shop at the end of our road. It was heartbreaking. Even so, I just could not part with some of my earliest childhood memories and so some of my favourite children's books are still stored in a box in my elderly Aunt's garage in the UK.

How I regretted it. Somehow I felt that our home had suddenly been stripped bare of its treasures and within a few weeks I began to collect another small collection from several of the English bookshops in the Costa Blanca, or from one of the many car boot sales that were springing up in the area.

Fortunately, before I had time to collect too many books we were on our travels again - this time to the Canary Islands. The cost of freight and the necessity of living in a small apartment for the first few months meant that the cruel process of disposing of books had to begin all over again.

In some ways, the lack of bookshops catering for the English speaking market in the Canary Islands has been a blessing because of the removal of temptation. Yes, I can buy books from car boot sales, charity stalls and the like, but somehow that doesn't have quite the same appeal as peaceful browsing in a bookshop.

So, it has had to be browsing online from Internet bookshops and then hoping that the book ordered eventually arrives in the post, or to wait until the next visit back to the UK. My reading for pleasure days seemed almost to be over until I discovered Kindle.

Kindle from Amazon is one of a number of remarkably clever devices from many manufacturers, and is marketed as an eBook reader. These devices are able to download a large number of books via the Internet, and many of the classics are free. My own eReader will store around 4000 books; so plenty to take away on holiday!

The choice of books is incredible and I personally find them easier to read on the eyes than a traditional paperback, because the size of text can be adjusted to suit personal taste. If you don't feel like reading, then an eBook reader can read the text to you! I can read books loaded into the eReader in bright sunlight or in darkness by using the light built into the case. I have already downloaded the complete collection of Charles Dickens and Thomas Hardy for the grand sum of 72 pence for each collection, as well as books from a number of modern authors, including the latest best sellers and thrillers.

As an expat living on an island, with little in the way of English language bookshops on hand, purchasing an eBook reader has been one of my best finds, and one that I highly recommend. Indeed, I have to confess to some self-interest, as I have recently published my own books in this format - a great way for me to combine my love of writing, as well as my love of gadgets!

For the traditionalists, that lovely smell of a new book is missing with an eBook, of course; neither is there that special feel of the crispness of paper, nor a shiny new book jacket, or the stiffness protecting an unopened book. However, if it is content that you are interested in, as well as the opportunity to escape into another world, then I can highly recommend it.

Expat Television

A recent announcement by the Chinese Government to axe more than two-thirds of prime time light entertainment shows and replace them with news broadcasts came as a shock to many, and was met with concern about further curbs on the freedom of the Chinese people.

This law to curb "excessive entertainment" on television is designed to reduce the number of scheduled entertainment programmes from 126 a week to just 38. However, after looking at Spanish television's uninspiring offerings for the current week, I began to wonder if this was actually quite an inspired move.

The true value and quality of the UK's BBC is only really appreciated once you have left the country. Arguments about licence fees, the quality of programming and schedules disappear into insignificance once you have left the country and realise that you can no longer receive its offerings.

Despite its faults, few will complain about the high quality of the national broadcaster's documentaries, news output and period dramas. It is one of those very British of institutions, like the British Heath Service, which has in many ways woven itself into the very fabric of what it is to be British. The BBC does not hold the monopoly on quality, of course, with ITV, Channel Four and even Sky TV producing some excellent programmes.

When I left the UK for Spain's Costa Blanca I resolutely decided that I would no longer care about what happened in "Corrie", or in Eastender's Queen Vic pub, for that matter.

Instead, I would content myself with all things Spanish, spend lazy evenings on the terrace, a glass of good wine in my hand, reading a good book or maybe focus on those initial attempts to learn the language and maybe the Spanish guitar! It was to be a whole new way of life, and one where television would not play a part.

How wrong I was! Within weeks of arriving at our new home, I was, along with all our neighbours, trying to find out the best ways of getting British television. We were surrounded by a motley collection of satellite dishes and a kind of baking tray contraption strapped to many rooftops, designed to receive micromesh re-transmission of UK television programmes.

At this point I will deftly step aside from the legal issues and arguments surrounding such contraptions, as it can lead to some difficulties. All in all, the Costa Blanca had the problem sorted. One way or another, British TV was easily available and was satisfying the needs of a growing expat population who were desperate to maintain links with 'home'.

Moving to the Canary Islands was a different matter. No longer were micromesh installations available, and satellite reception required a massive dish to receive the questionable delights of Sky TV.

Indeed, I had a neighbour who filled almost the entirety of his front garden with the largest satellite dish that I have ever seen for a home installation. (I understand that the both the European Space Agency and the Island's airport are very interested in renting bandwidth!) With the advent of Internet television and the BBC's iPlayer, it is clear that British television is a must for most expats and, despite the best efforts of UK authorities to prevent receiving transmissions overseas, given a little time and effort, there are always ways around the problem.

I am often asked why there is such a demand for British television. Apart from the obvious answer of keeping in touch with our country of birth and programmes in a language that can be easily understood, the reason is very simple. In the main, most Spanish television programmes are of poor quality.

With the exception of some very good news coverage, most schedules are filled with American movies, quiz and chat shows, as well␣␣␣that beast to be avoided at all costs, reality television. Period dramas, for instance, rarely feature in the schedules.

Maybe China's decision to axe much of the content on its channels is desirable, or is it yet another attempt by the state to control? I guess the human rights people will be discussing this issue in the weeks to come; meanwhile I am going to enjoy the next episode of Eastenders!

Go Virtual

I am often surprised that many expats have never heard of a Virtual Private Network (VPN). I have managed to watch television channels, which I am not supposed to watch as I am living outside the UK, for many years without a satellite dish or expensive television retransmission service, just by hooking up my TV to a second computer and watching by courtesy of the Internet.

Yes, the quality of reception has been very variable and I have been plagued by 'low bandwidth issues', although please don't ask me what this is, because I really don't have a clue, technically speaking. All I know is that the Internet signal is a bit like a running stream, and if you are at the end of the line or with a service provider who restricts your flow, you end up with little more than a dribble.

This is the problem that I had for a number of years in Spain, until I changed Internet service providers. Magic, the flow became a torrent and I now rarely suffer from the curse of 'buffering'.

Watching television programmes from the UK, bypassing all forms of geographical restrictions, accessing blocked sites, just because you happen to be an expat living in another country, bypassing Internet 'security' monitors, unblocking access to YouTube, Skype and television channels, as well as the encryption of all of your Internet traffic, suddenly becomes possible with a Virtual Private Network.

So, what is a Virtual Private Network? If you look up the subject on Google, Wikipedia or similar, you will find very complicated explanations. In simple terms, it is basically a system that uses the Internet to connect to remote sites in another country.

VPN uses 'virtual' connections that are routed through the Internet to connect to remote sites, which immediately enables access to services provided only in that country.

A Virtual Private Network suddenly provides open communication across countries and political barriers, just as the Internet was originally meant to be by its founder. Many countries and companies are constantly trying to restrict what can be seen by the general public, and based purely upon where you are.

With VPN you can unblock streaming services, such as favourite television stations and gaming and lottery sites, by accessing servers in their broadcast areas, such as from your country of origin.

Internet security is also a troubling issue nowadays. I make a point that whenever I access my online bank accounts, both in Spain and in the UK, I divert my Internet access though VPN, which makes financial transactions private and more secure with encryption.

Having a VPN is just another small way that you can help to defeat the all watching eyes of 'Big Brother', and open up greater enjoyment from the Internet as an expat.

The VPN service is also remarkably cheap for the benefits it offers. I have used a number of free services in the past, but these were inevitably unreliable, as many services were directed through Asian servers, which seemed to me an unnecessarily long way for the signal to travel!

Instead, for a number of years, I have used a service that is based in the UK, and for which I pay about £5 per month. For me, the VPN service is worth every penny. The price too has remained constant over the years and, most importantly, has been totally reliable. Personally, I wouldn't be without it.

For further information about this and other VPN providers, as well as other useful information, have a look at the Expat Survival section of my website.

A Connection at the Mortuary

One of the downsides of living in a remote area is the problem with mobile phone signals. Although I live reasonably close to a large town, by the time that I get to the village where we live, the signal from all the major networks has all but disappeared.

It is not unusual to see and hear neighbours lurking at the end of their roads, angrily shouting loudly into their mobiles in a desperate attempt to allow the person at the other end to hear what they are saying. Needless to say, shouting does not work, but it does make life interesting for the neighbours!

As the mobile phone signal is so poor, it is easy to see that Internet data connection to send emails by using a mobile phone is almost impossible. I have tried so many times to achieve a blue flashing light on my modem in an attempt to hold a data transfer signal for more than a few seconds, with little success.

It all came to a head during the recent storms. Thunder, lightning, heavy rain and gale force winds soon knocked out our electricity supply and the telephone connection, complete with Internet broadband connection.

Since leaving the UK, I have come to realise that a good Internet connection is one of the essentials of life and vital for maintaining links with family and friends in other parts of the world via Skype, email and for the multiplicity of online tasks that many of us take for granted nowadays.

There was no Internet and no electricity and I had an urgent email to send to meet a deadline for one of the publications that I write for. I thought that a journey to the nearest commercial centre would be a good idea; after all they offer free Wi-Fi access.

A difficult journey across flooded roads proved to be of no use. No, their Internet connection was not working either. I tried several cafe bars in the town, as well as lurking outside a house of ill repute, which does have the virtue of an open Internet connection 24 hours a day - no doubt to meet the needs of their clients! I'm not fussy, by now I was desperate for a connection - whatever the source. Sadly, Donna's House of Sinful Pleasures was not connected either!

Finally, I had an idea! I remembered that I had once managed to achieve a respectable signal outside the local mortuary. I grabbed my laptop computer, the appropriate dongle (a clever thing that works a bit like a mobile phone to send and receive data signals) and headed off in the rain, wind and dark to the forbidding building outside my village - not a place to be on a wet, dark and stormy night.

Once in the car park, I managed to climb onto a boulder and strap the dongle to a nearby post and link it with a long cable to the laptop computer in the car. After a few anxious moments, the modem burst into life, the blue light flashed and I was at last able to send my contribution to the magazine in time to meet the deadline.

I do hope that in time, the mobile phone companies will improve the strength of the signal to my village, but, meanwhile, I always have the mortuary to help me out in a crisis!

Food and Drink

The Vegetarian Expat

I have been a vegetarian for many years. I was a vegetarian when it was seen as cranky, receiving comments such as, "Are you sure you can live without meat?" to the time when vegetarianism became the thing for weight loss, or as a declaration by students, mainly to annoy their parents. It then became fashionable to be vegetarian; later, it was definitely for the health conscious, and now vegetarianism is seen as the way to conserve the world's scarce food resources.

My personal reason for becoming vegetarian so many years ago was very simple; I like animals and I do not wish to eat my friends.

Living in a remote part of Lincolnshire, with few children of my own age to play with, no doubt encouraged me to develop a friendship with animals in such a way that I could not bear to eat their flesh. I shall always be grateful to my parents for having a very liberal view in allowing me to keep all kinds of animals, birds, reptiles and insects as pets.

As long as I could demonstrate that I was responsible enough to care for them properly, my parents accepted most of the livestock that I brought home without putting up too much resistance. I have many happy memories of my father building hutches for rabbits and guinea pigs, as well as cages, runs and even a large aviary for a multitude of birds that came my way.

My mother was always on duty as chief nurse should one of my furry or feathered friends develop an illness of some kind, and very good at it she was too. However, even she declined to give my hamster the kiss of life, despite my insistence, when I discovered him lifeless in his cage one morning.

However, I am pleased to report that with a spot of heart massage and a teaspoonful of brandy, my furry friend was soon up and about again, if a little groggy. Maybe this early encounter explains my love affair with a decent cognac after a good meal.

Moving to Spain was a shock in many ways, including the difficulties in explaining vegetarianism to many waiters. Gone were the days when the flippant comment, "I don't eat anything with a face or a mother," was a sufficient explanation as in the UK. Yes, I know all about the egg issue.

The problem was that most Spanish and Canarians were, and some still are, convinced that tuna is a vegetable; it does not count as meat or fish. Despite my well practiced explanation of "sin carne, sin pescado" (no meat or fish) I can guarantee that most salads usually arrive with a generous dollop of tuna in the centre, and in some cases, the salad is liberally sprinkled with ham.

I blame most of this on the "I'm a vegetarian, but I eat fish and chicken" brigade, who do no service to either themselves or the vegetarian cause.

This part of life when moving to the Costa Blanca was a culinary nightmare for the unsuspecting vegetarian, later eased by the few British supermarkets that had identified a lucrative market. It was now possible to easily obtain soya, tofu, nut roll and my old favourite, Linda McCartney sausages.

We even managed to obtain vegetarian dog food via a tortuous route and, judging from the good health of our dogs over the years, this put paid to the 'special diet' syndrome that so many vets are forcing on to an unsuspecting public nowadays.

All this changed when we moved to the Canary Islands. Gone once again was the ease of availability of so many products that we had taken for granted in the Costa Blanca. British supermarkets came and went, and the reliability of a regular source of vegetable protein could not be taken for granted.

Thankfully, we discovered a Canarian favourite, gofio, flour derived from maize, which is a traditional dish and served in many ways. In days gone by, farmers also used it to feed to their dogs and now we enjoy it too. If you look at the menu of many traditional Canarian restaurants, you will see it as a popular, creamy dessert.

However, we bake it, fry it and grill it. We even have it sliced cold, rather like a nut roast and even barbecue it. Prepared carefully, and flavoured with the right herbs and spices, it is delicious!

Space is too short to include a recipe here, but you will find one on the Expat Survival section of my website.

Fit to drink?

A recent announcement by Thames Water in London announcing that polluted water from the River Thames is to be cleaned sufficiently to provide drinking water for the population of London surprised me. Not only is this initiative the UK's first major attempt to desalinate water, but it is also claimed to be new technology, which it isn't.

The Thames Gateway water treatment works in Beckton, East London cost around £270m to build and was brought into service in 2010. However, the company has only recently got around to testing it fully in recent weeks and during the recent 'hot spell' in the UK.

The 875 million litres proudly produced by the plant so far is said to be really clean and, reassuringly, is treated with salts and other chemicals to make it taste roughly the same as that lovely Thames tap water.

It is claimed that the technology is mostly used in the Middle East, and only after Thames Water successfully made the case that new sources of water are needed, with climate change bringing hotter, drier summers, as well as an increasing population moving into the capital.

London has less annual rainfall than cities such as Sydney and Athens, and is classified as "seriously water-stressed" by the UK's Environment Agency.

However, some have claimed that water desalination is wasteful of energy and unsustainable and it would be much better to pipe water to the capital from Scotland and Wales.

It also appears that if all the leaks in the Thames Water supply system were plugged, around 26 per cent of water would be saved. It seems that reducing leakage by just 1% would provide enough water for almost 250,000 people; an interesting statistic.

Meanwhile, many of my friends and relatives in the UK are complaining of hosepipe bans and restrictions to watering the garden and washing the car. Despite criticism of water desalination in the UK, there are now 15,180 major desalination plants in 150 countries, supplying about 300 million people with water each day.

Many of these plants are in the Middle East, as well as the USA and Spain and, of course, the Canary Islands. After all, we are surrounded by the stuff, and plenty of wind, so it is sensible to make good use of it.

In the years that I have lived in the Canary Islands, I have never known a water shortage or a ban on using hosepipes. Yes, we have desalination plants not, incidentally, cleansing water from a grubby River Thames, but from seawater.

As for wasting energy, the desalination plant near to my home in Pozo Izquierdo uses the excess electricity generated from the wind turbines to provide power for the adjacent desalination plant.

How about wind and seawater? I seem to remember that there is plenty of both somewhere near the Thames.

Just a Trifle

Who likes trifle? It is strange how the Christmas and New Year period reminds us of earlier times. I guess that as we get older, incidents and memories that seemed so unimportant and irrelevant to us years ago, gain in both colour and importance as time passes. For me, one of these delightful memories is my Mum's Christmas trifle.

I have rarely thought about trifle since moving to Spain and the Canary Islands but, this Christmas, I had a craving for the one that my Mum used to make. Although my Mum died many years ago, it is true that memories of people we loved live on in so many different ways.

Mum's trifle will be one those special memories, and not unique to me, that so many of us of a certain age will remember. I am not talking about one of those instant factory-made chemical concoctions that we often find lingering in chiller cabinets in the large UK supermarkets nowadays, but a real trifle painstaking made from layers of tinned fruit, sponge cakes (remember those?), red jelly and Bird's custard (yes, it had to be Bird's!).

Depending upon the celebration and time of year, it would be topped with sprinklings of tiny 'hundreds and thousands' and tiny silver balls for Christmas, little sugar eggs for Easter and so on. The content was always the same and gloriously predictable, as would my Dad's comments be about the sherry. Yes, the secret ingredient was always Mum's very generous dose of sweet sherry!

As a 'non-drinker' and someone who had 'signed the pledge' as a child, Mum used to keep a few bottles of essential booze in the cupboard for "medicinal purposes only". It was strange that I never remember being offered any when I was ill, but I do remember that most of the bottles had to be replaced from time to time, which I thought very odd.

Mum's special addition to the Christmas trifle would always be criticised by my father as "heavy handed", although it was clear that he, my brothers and I used to thoroughly enjoy it. I have not tasted one like it for many years.

My longing for trifle was resolved this Christmas. I happened to mention my loss to the elderly mother of a friend, Gloria, who was visiting our island for a pre-Christmas break. Her eyes lit up when I mentioned Mum's special trifle. It was clear that Gloria knew exactly what I was talking about. "I'll make you one," Gloria announced.

True to her word, we visited our friend and Gloria again just before they were leaving for the UK. A dish of freshly made trifle duly appeared with Gloria watching my every expression as I ate the first spoonful. It was delicious! More importantly, it really was my Mum's trifle, made with the same ingredients and expertise that Mum had used all those years ago. Somehow, all the Christmases past seemed to merge together and in an instant I was transported back to many years earlier. Thank you, Gloria, and thanks Mum!

A Mince Pie for Christmas

It is strange how expats suddenly develop a craving for something that reminds them of life in their countries of origin. I guess it is not that surprising really, as Christmas is the time of year when our memories, particularly as we get older, recall times gone by, both happy and sad.

Many of those special times have occurred, of course, over the Christmas and New Year period; many of us will have fond memories of families and friends, of precious times spent together, unique family traditions, gifts and special food that appeared at this time of the year.

Since moving to Spain, I seem to have developed a craving for mince pies. When we lived in the UK, I would not give a mince pie the time of day; similarly Christmas puddings, which I always used to consider to be a total waste of space and time.

Why one would consume a hearty Christmas dinner, only to be followed by a plateful of thick brown stodge and custard was beyond me. I would only ever eat a spoonful of pudding to please my mother, who had made several during the summer months.

You see, mother's Christmas pudding making was a family tradition, a legend, and I can still see the huge copper boiler steaming away for what seemed like hours, as she prepared puddings for Christmas Day, Boxing Day and for each of my brother's and my own birthdays.

This activity took place each summer; she did not freeze them and, I am told, they became even more delicious as the months went by.

I have since learned that this was due to my mother's generosity in a liberal application from the newly opened bottle of brandy that was part of the creation of this annual treat. I guess it was a basic form of embalming!

Last year, a neighbour appeared at our gate a week before Christmas, begging for help in obtaining a supply of mince pies for her Christmas party. We made a few suggestions and she went away determined to track down a few boxes. Unlike in previous years, we had also found great difficulty in locating mince pies, and we crossed our fingers that our suggestions would be helpful and that it would help the party to go with a swing.

A few days later, our neighbour spotted us, waved and beamed. Yes, she had tracked down two boxes of mince pies - the last on the island, it seemed.

This year we went to our nearest branch of Marks and Spencer. Although a franchise of the UK store, stocking only a limited range of foodstuffs, we were very hopeful of finding some as we had allowed plenty of time before Christmas. The friendly sales assistant shook her head sadly, "No, we have none left," she said. She noticed our disappointment and added, "I can get you some if you like."

She picked up the phone with a flourish and called the main branch in Las Palmas and handed the phone to us. I spoke to a very helpful lady in Las Palmas, who confirmed that she had two boxes left and would send them down to our local store the following day. How's that for service?

We now have our mince pies, and very nice they are too! I can already hear some of you thinking, "Why don't you make your own?" Fair point, but have you tried getting a supply of mincemeat over here? Believe me, trying to explain such an item, in Spanish to bemused sales staff, really is not worth the trouble, but I will leave that story for another time!

Baking Bread

Expats in many countries, and particularly those in Spain, Portugal and France, will quickly discover many wonderful bakeries. Forget the plastic bread on sale in the supermarkets, but that wonderful bread baked in relatively small quantities by people who recognise that it is the taste of real bread that buyers are looking for. I like a simple, freshly baked loaf of bread, preferably white and with a dark and crispy crust.

However, I still cannot quite find the taste and texture of the loaf that I was used to in the UK, despite having a wonderful bakery in the village where all types of loaves are baked.

I am pleased that I had the foresight to pack the bread maker when we left the UK. I had tried several models over the years, and all failed after a few months; it was friends who recommended a model made by Panasonic.

Twelve years later, the bread-maker is still producing two or three loaves a week, with additional loaves made for friends and neighbours. The smell of freshly baked bread really is one of the most appetising of aromas, and is to be highly recommended if you are entertaining, or trying to sell your property!

Two months ago, our trusty bread-maker developed a strange grating noise. Twelve years of faithful baking was a reasonable lifespan in an age when planned obsolescence seems to be the current norm, and so I ordered a replacement machine from Amazon.

A week later, a huge box arrived with the replacement machine. In many ways, the new machine looked very similar to the old one and baked a perfect loaf of bread the first time that I used it.

Before disposing of the old machine, I gave it a good shake. I heard something click inside, and I felt the need to give it just one more try. I added all the ingredients and the four-hour process began. It now appeared to be working perfectly, with no grating noise. It too made a perfect loaf of bread, so clearly a good shake was the answer!

We now have two bread-makers in our house. Some may think it strange or maybe obsessive, but I have found it to be a real advantage as I can now bake two loaves of bread at the same time. I can open only one packet of yeast and flour without any waste, and the job is done and forgotten for another week.

Another advantage is that I am in control of the ingredients. There are no added preservatives and salt and sugar are kept to a minimum, unlike loaves purchased in the supermarkets. Also, bread is very cheap to make at home, which is another advantage during these difficult financial times.

Yeast has been difficult to find in Spain and the Canary Islands. Bread-making machines are not that popular over here, and most home bakers use fresh yeast from their local bakery.

This is not advised for use in bread-making machines and dried yeast is hard to find. I usually rely on thoughtful friends bringing a supply of yeast from Tesco or Sainsburys in the UK, although in an emergency I can get an expensive supply from the El Corte Ingles department store.

During my first hesitant attempts at bread making in the Canary Islands, I used 'levadura en polvo', which I thought was dried yeast. The dreadful result sent me heading for the dictionary, where I discovered that 'levadura en polvo' is actually baking powder. What I really needed was 'levadura de panadero', which is bakers yeast.

If you are also tempted to bake your own bread, have a look at the 'Expat Survival' section of my website, where I have included further details. Bella (our dog) and I are just off for morning coffee, toast and Marmite!

Fancy a Cup of Coffee?

One of the many things that I enjoy about living in the Canary Islands is a decent cup of coffee. Gone are the days when "a cup of instant" seemed to be the norm, and I still shudder when I return to the UK for a brief visit. A visit to one of the relatively new, and supposedly trendy, overpriced coffee shops is, for me, an ordeal best avoided.

A quick visit out of sheer desperation during a frantic shopping expedition led me into one of the many branches of 'Costa Lottee' that are opening up in all of the UK's High Streets - after all, it did offer "Free Wi-Fi Connection."

My request for a cup of black coffee, no I don't like mugs, was met with a disinterested look as the spotty youth pointed to a huge variety of coffees on the board above his sentry post.

"Take yer pick," he slurped, as he continued chewing his gum and picking his finger nail.

"That one will do," I replied, "but I only want a small cup and not a mugful."

"We only do them mugs," he replied stabbing at the nearest soup bowl with a fingernail partly hanging from his index finger.

"But I only want a small cup...," I protested.

Realising that discussion with the spotty youth was pointless, I handed over my £3.50 and perched myself on a most uncomfortable stool at the side of an equally unfortunate table with three legs - goodness, they still do Formica!

Maybe I should count myself fortunate that the loose fingernail was not floating in my coffee... The coffee was one of the most revolting drinks that I have ever tasted. Two sips and I was gone.

I contrast this with a cafe bar in my nearest town, Vecindario, on the island. It is a real town with real people, and well away from the expensive bars in the south of the island. Here I can get a cup of excellent coffee for 90 cents, sit in comfort and people-watch for as long as I wish.

I watch Canarians, Spanish, Chinese, Russians, Germans, Scandinavians, Africans and Indians pass by, together with a variety of skin colour, clothing and headgear. It makes me realise once again that I am living in a community where race, colour, faith and language rarely matter. It is a community where most people just get on with each other and I know how fortunate I am.

Back to my cup of coffee. Did you know that coffee is grown in Gran Canaria, as it has been since 1788 when King Carlos III issued a decree ordering the introduction of the first coffee plants to the Island?

Today, coffee is produced in very small amounts by local farmers who have kept the tradition of growing and consuming the coffee that they produce for many generations. The coffee is called Finca la Corcovada and is grown in the Valley of Agaete. This valley has a microclimate and a rich soil, perfect for growing coffee, and is grown by Juan Godoy, the only coffee grower in Europe and who is now supplying the UK market.

My memory returns to Costa Lottee in the UK, and the spotty youth who is, no doubt, still filling his soup-bowl mugs with foul-tasting overpriced coffee. I wonder if he will be serving coffee from Gran Canaria?

Marmite and Mosquitoes

Regular readers of 'Letters from the Atlantic' will remember that I am a great fan of Marmite. Yes, I readily accept that Marmite is rather like Blackpool or Benidorm - you either love it or hate it; in my case, I like all three. This 'Letter' concerns my recent discovery about the thwarting of these miserable little beasts, mosquitoes, with a healthy dose of Marmite.

No, I am not suggesting that you cover your bodies with a layer of the black stuff; although I am sure it would be highly effective, it may be going a little too far and you would not be too popular at parties.

When we first moved to Spain we lived very close to the salt lakes in the Costa Blanca. We quickly discovered that, at certain times of the year, attacks from mosquitoes were part of life and, as a result, mosquito blinds and nets were quickly installed in our home.

I recall spending a miserable few months with my arms and legs covered with itching, red spots that took weeks to disappear. I spent hot summer evenings on our sun terrace, relaxing and enjoying a few drinks with neighbours - wrapped from head to toes in clothing designed to cover all parts of my body; I even wore long socks pulled over my long trousers. This was not quite how I had imagined life in sunny Spain. Despite these precautions I was badly bitten; the little 'perishers' clearly adored the taste of me.

Others were much more fortunate. My partner and many friends were rarely attacked, whilst others were, and it seemed that it was individual odour that mosquitoes were attracted to. Indeed, it seems that mosquitoes avoid around ten per cent of the human population, because they simply do not like their smell, and so I regard it as a compliment.

We invested heavily in sprays and creams, whilst the usual bar chat claimed that it was alcohol in the blood that mosquitoes sensed and liked, and that they preferred some drinks to others! Well, I was certainly not going to change my favourite tipple just for them.

Moving to the Canary Islands, I was initially troubled by a few bites, although nowhere near as bad as in the Costa Blanca. However, after a few months right up to the present time, I am rarely bitten at all.

This puzzled me until after listening to a recent radio programme and reading some of the latest research on the subject from a team who are designing new products to combat mosquitoes' voracious appetites. This revealed that one of the things that mosquitoes dislike is the smell, and presumably the taste, of vitamin B12. It was at this point that all became clear.

In the UK I would eat Marmite regularly. However, moving to the Costa Blanca meant that there were no ready supplies available. There were more important things to do, such as getting a water and electricity supply, and so my passion for Marmite lapsed temporarily.

However, after moving to the Canary Islands, we discovered a ready supply in our local supermarket and I started eating toast and Marmite again each day for my elevenses. Our dog, Bella, enjoys it too and always demands one 'soldier' and sulks if I forget. So what was the link? Well, it seems that as Marmite is rich in vitamin B12, this is acting as a mosquito repellent.

It seems that although there are many Marmite lovers and haters around the world, our mosquito friends really do detest the stuff! Readers may have their own strategies for dealing with the problem of mosquitoes; if so, do please let me know.

Political

Voting in Spain and the Canary Islands

I am no expert on constitutional affairs, but I have watched the shenanigans in the UK with increasing incredulity. I think I have missed a chapter somewhere, but I cannot see why AV (alternative vote) was recommended to voters, when it seems to be widely recognised as a flawed system, now clearly seen by voters as worse than the current 'first past the post' system.

This brings me to the forthcoming local elections in Spain and the Canary Islands. Sadly, there is no Nick Clegg to wind up here, just a basic system of proportional representation, which seems to work rather well.

I have made up my mind to vote either for the male candidate who has the least facial hair, or for the woman who looks least like a poorly prepared drag queen. Another factor for me to consider is that I shall immediately disqualify any candidate who hires one of those noisy loudspeaker vans that drives past our house so fast with their distorted loudspeaker systems that I cannot understand a word that they are saying.

Bella hates it and barks and cries loudly, whilst Mackitten meows pure vengeance. Those speaker vans disturb the usual tranquillity of our neighbourhood and have a lot to answer for. I am sometimes asked about the voting system in Spain, so I thought it would be useful to write a 'Letter' about it.

Voting here is by proportional representation, with each party publishing a list of candidates equal to the number of councillor seats available in the municipality. Councillors are elected in proportion to the total votes that they have won.

If, for instance, a municipality has 17 councillors to be elected, a party that wins 65% of the total votes will have 9 councillors and be able to govern without forming a coalition because they have won a majority.

If no party wins a majority, minority parties can form a coalition government grouping that may even exclude the 'winning party'. It is therefore important under PR that everyone who believes in the policies of a particular party votes.

One danger of PR is that the party that receives the highest number of votes can actually be completely excluded from government if a coalition of minority parties can be formed.

So how do we vote? On Election Day, you need to take your identification with a photo (a passport usually puts paid to any arguments about ID cards and driving licences!) and the voting paper for the party that you wish to vote for in the envelope to the polling station.

Remember too that you are voting for a party and not a person, unlike in the UK.

Most political parties will already have sent voters their own voting papers and an envelope before polling day. You need to ensure that you have placed the correct voting paper in the envelope and take it to the polling station.

Don't be tempted to write on the voting paper, even an 'X' will be disqualified, as will any rude comments about the candidates!

Even if you don't have a voting paper before polling day, you can still go to the polling station, go to the polling booth, and select one paper for the party that you fancy, place it in the envelope and seal it. You then go to the desk, show your passport and hand the envelope to the clerk at the desk who will put it in the box. That's it; democracy has been seen to be done! Now, no more talk of AV, Coalitions or Nick Clegg until next time!

Flamenco - the latest weapon!

Recently we have heard about protests in the UK, whether these are students campaigning against the increase in university tuition fees or anti-capitalist groups and other protestors taking direct action against what they see as injustice. Others are holding 'sit-ins' in the stores of a mobile telephone company or those owned by a government advisor, whose wife happens to live outside the UK, allegedly for the purpose of avoiding taxation.

It seems that the days are gone when planned protest marches were the province of well-organised trade unions fighting for what they see as just causes for their members. Nowadays we see students and others taking direct action by attacking the headquarters of political parties, banks and government buildings.

Protests organised through social networking groups have led to spontaneous protests in well-known UK shops and stores by protestors who see them as legitimate targets for not always peaceful protests.

As with many things, the Spanish do this in another way, and maybe this illustrates just one side of the Spanish psyche that I find fascinating, charming, and often amusing, in my adopted country. A new craze by Spain's anti-bank protestors is sweeping the nation.

As an alternative to the angry UK's direct-action protestors that are engaged in street violence or fire bombing offices, angry citizens in Spain are calling into banks and dancing a live flamenco show, complete with anti-bank lyrics before disappearing as quickly as they arrived.

These groups of people are spontaneously called together for an anti-bank protest by an anonymous umbrella group called Flo6x8 Flashmob. The group gives the participants the lyrics and rhythms of the songs to sing and then let the protestors visit local bank branches to carry out their protests in their own individual styles.

The groups usually scatter euro cent coins on the floor in protest at the bank's 'penny pinching' approach to the recession. The umbrella group's only stipulation is that the flamenco must be 'good flamenco'. There will usually be a central dancer backed up by a rhythm group to provide the harmonisation, and by all accounts their performances are not only entertaining, but appear to make their point very effectively.

Currently, banks and police are unsure about how best to deal with these protests, but these groups seem to be getting their message across. Maybe the angry students demonstrating against increased university fees, and the anti-taxation dodger groups who are currently targeting popular stores may wish to consider this entertaining and very Spanish form of protest on future occasions?

Getting into hot water

Listening to the UK Prime Minister and the Energy Minister's attempts to help consumers with their fuel bills this year brought a mixture of indignation, amusement and cynicism from many UK consumers. Some would say that the issue cannot truly be resolved simply by endlessly switching energy companies and tariffs, together with the odd roll of loft insulation.

Many have commented that these regurgitated suggestions are akin to a sticking plaster being offered to a dying patient. Energy experts tell us that the root cause has more to do with the rising cost of oil, greater demand for energy from China and India, diminishing oil supplies, the financial crisis, as well as the excessive profiteering made by greedy energy companies operating within a distorted market.

The problem of rising fuel bills will take much more than a one day meeting chaired by the Prime Minister, slick press conferences and bright orange publicity posters to drag this particular patient from his death throes.

So, how about green energy and renewables? Dare I even mention wind turbines for fear of middle England starting yet another petition against them and complaining in the Daily Mail?

Politicians of all shades appear to subscribe to the cause, task forces are set up to produce endless policy documents about the subject, whilst others are happily considering drilling for shale oil, together with the associated risks of poisoning water supplies, as well as having another go at blowing up Blackpool in the process. Yes, that minor earthquake a few months ago was not "natural" and was apparently due to initial drilling for shale oil in the area.

Some thirty years ago I had friends in Dorset who had the good sense to install four solar panels to the roof of their bungalow. In those days it was considered unusual, if not a little eccentric. However, our friends used the hot water provided by the sun for most of the year, topped up occasionally by an immersion heater when there was a sudden demand for consecutive hot baths when visitors came to stay. If it works in Dorset for most of the year, why not in the Canary Islands?

The Canary Islands are at the forefront of solar technology and Spain itself is a pioneer in solar power development. Our climate is ideal as the Canary Islands are one of the most highly exposed sun regions of the world.

There are currently solar projects subsidised by the Canary Islands' Government and fully backed by the Government of Spain. However, I see very few solar installations on either domestic or business premises in the Canary Islands, and I don't understand why this is.

Several years ago we were interested in buying a new property that came with the option of fitted solar panels as an extra. I discussed this with the builder who, although anxious to complete the sale, was less enthusiastic about fitting solar panels.

According to the builder, solar panels caused considerable problems after installation because of the high use of desalinated water on the island; he claimed that it led to corrosion. Now, I am not an expert on solar technology, but I know enough to recognise that there are different types of panels designed for different purposes and conditions, and it is merely a question of selecting the right one for the job.

Until the last few years, electricity bills were not a great concern in the Canary Islands, and energy prices in Spain were lower than in many other countries. A cooler night in February usually results in lighting a few candles for a little additional warmth, and we would think we had a harsh winter if we switched on our electric radiator for more than a few evenings. However, air conditioning is another matter, and high consumption soon results in a large bill.

Energy prices have since rocketed for all of us in recent years, and we need to take energy issues much more seriously by fully utilising our natural 'green' resources, such as the wind, waves and sun.

Maybe our politicians should focus less on 'sticking plaster policies' and expensive "Switch" publicity campaigns, and much more on actually solving a developing problem.

The European Family

I admit to being a proud European. Although English born and bred, and I still love the United Kingdom, including Scotland if it remains within the Union, I do not regard myself as English or British, but European. I know it is not a particularly popular concept at the present time, but I am proud to be European.

Just mention the EU to most Brits and you will probably be greeted by a shrug or a scowl; it is often regarded as a necessary evil, at worst, and as the price to be paid for being part of one of the World's largest trading blocks, at best.

Major infrastructure projects, which have received considerable funding from the EU, usually prefer to ignore that minor fact.

I contrast this to Spain and the Canary Islands where projects, both large and small, proudly announce that they are funded by the EU, and usually fly three flags, the Spanish flag, the Canary Islands flag, as well as the European Union flag.

Speaking to a British expat the other day made me realise the depth of the problem. He has lived and worked in the Canary Islands and Spain for about thirty years, but resents the fact that Polish workers, as well as other East European citizens, are now living and working in his home town in the UK.

He quite readily accepted the fact that being in the European Union as a British expat means that he can live and work in Spain, or any country within the EU, without the need for a visa or work permit, but resented that benefit being given to workers from other European countries. He could not accept the logic and we agreed to disagree about the issue.

I am also a firm believer in the euro, again a concept that is currently out of favour, even though several new members of the EU still aspire to join the euro one day. Memories are short and hindsight is a wonderful thing, but it is not that long ago when UK politicians were endorsing the project with great enthusiasm.

The "I told you so" brigade are currently having a wonderful time, reminding the populace they always thought it was a bad idea. Yes, we know the euro monetary system has its flaws, and Greece is currently paying the price of a process that did not apply or stick to the rules that were established at its formation, but the idea of a currency that can be used anywhere in Europe is still, to my mind, a wonderful concept.

Now back to my euro-sceptic friend. He firmly believes that having one currency has taken the personality and excitement from travelling to other countries. He much prefers a Europe whereby he has to carry at least six different currencies for a two-week holiday.

No, he doesn't mind being ripped off with high exchange rate charges, nor does he mind losing the value of the remaining currency when he returns home. After all, that suitcase of unspent pesetas, lira and drachmas would be of great interest to the grandchildren in the future, wouldn't they?

For me, this is only part of the story. The fact that I can choose to live and work in any country within the European Union, without a visa or work permit gives me a great sense of freedom, as well as belonging. Admittedly, the recession has recently led to some adjustments being made to the 'free movement' principle in some European countries, but the basic principle remains.

I can benefit from healthcare, employment, trading and human rights laws that are common to all members of the EU. It comes with a form of protection; a reassurance of knowing that there is a common denominator that applies to all regardless of whether I am in a Scandinavian city or basking on a beach in the Canary Islands.

Of course, I am not naive enough to turn a blind eye to what is also an imperfect system, but it is the best we have. I have only to talk to friends and colleagues from the US and other parts of the world, to realise that we are part of something very special, which is the envy of much of the world.

So, to my euro-sceptic friend, I say, of course, there needs to be continual improvement and change within the EU, because it is an evolving project that must adapt to the needs of its people. However, the post war dream of our forefathers, of a Europe, working together in friendship and cooperation for the mutual benefit of all, is an ideal that is still worth striving for.

Fluffy Tales

A Kitten in the Canaries

Regular readers of 'Letters from the Atlantic' may recall that an emaciated, flea ridden and sickly kitten burst into my life last year, and a number of readers have been asking about what happened to him.

Although I like all animals, maybe with the exception of snakes, I had no intention of allowing a cat to take up residence in our home. I saw myself as, first and foremost, a dog lover; I understand them and always have had at least one dog by my side. I liked cats too, but had no understanding of them.

Also, I was nervous of having one because, on our island, there appears to be a policy of poisoning the stray cat population - they are regarded as vermin to be destroyed. In my own village, for example, there used to be many cats and now there are hardly any. Witnessing a child grieving over her poisoned cat in its death throws is not easy to forget.

Bella, our crazy little dog, found the kitten on wasteland during one of our walks. We took the tiny ball of fluff out of the baking sun and home to die in peace. A little water and a teaspoonful from a hastily purchased tin of cat food seemed to satisfy the little intruder, and he quickly fell asleep in a cardboard box that we found for him.

I remember holding the tiny scrap of life in the palm of my hand, and wishing him to live, but doubting that would happen.

The next morning I was up early, dreading opening the box and what I would find inside. Surprisingly, two large eyes stared at me and the kitten began to lick my fingers. I gave him a little more food, which he ate hungrily and licked the water droplets from my fingers.

Each day, Mac, as we named the tiny, furry intruder, after my love of all things Apple Mac, gradually grew in confidence and health. On one memorable day he began to purr and it was the sweetest sound. He nestled into my hand, whilst I tickled his head gently with my finger. I began to feel some hope.

A few days later we took Mac to the vet for a check up, but that gave us great concern. We were told that it is the law in the Canary Islands that stray kittens such as Mac have to have a blood test to check for HIV infection.

The vet did not say what would happen to him if the test was found to be positive. We feared the worst as we were told that HIV is common with stray cats in the Canary Islands.

The week long wait for the test results were to be long and harrowing, and I tried to detach myself from my growing affection for the kitten.

It was good news! Mac was pronounced as healthy, but needed nourishment and a great deal of care if he was to survive and grow into a healthy cat. By then our concern was that Mac would not play.

He showed no interest in fluffy toys, balls of wool and all the usual paraphernalia that we thought kittens adored. Phone calls to cat-loving friends began to raise concerns that Mac may be brain damaged; that he did not play, because he could not play. We refused to accept this possibility and began a process of teaching him to play. It took time, but we eventually succeeded.

Today, one year later, Mac has had his annual check up and injections and pronounced a "very fit and very healthy cat". We adore him, and even Bella seems happy to see him around, although she disapproves of him hiding and playing with her toys.

He is now a much-valued member of our family and because he is a house cat, spends much of his time on my desk when I am writing. I suspect he likes the heat from the desk lamp.

Annoyingly, he has a fetish for pens and pencils and is always stealing them. He is also very intelligent - far more intelligent than most of our dogs and he never ceases to amaze me with his skilful manipulation of life, as well as the people around him!

Mac has not only changed our lives, but also added so much to it. Little did I know on that fateful day in May last year, that a tiny worm- and flea-ridden ball of fluff could enrich our lives in so many ways.

Vets and Pets

Our little dog Bella, a lively, and slightly crazy mixture of something between a Papillion and fruit bat, recently developed a bad limp in one her back legs. We were not too concerned at first, particularly as we now also have a kitten, and Bella and Mac spend many hours playing together, and sometimes these games are a little over exuberant.

The problem also tends to occur every six months or so, and I am convinced that somehow it is linked to her menstruation cycle. Usually, the bad leg returns to normal after a week or two of rest.

This time the problem continued and we took Bella to the vet for an anti-inflammatory injection or tablets, which usually does the trick. The helpful young vet gave her a thorough examination and it was clear after all the probing and prodding that Bella was not in any pain.

The vet also suggested that he took a couple of X-rays to make sure that all was in order. The X-rays showed inflammation and the vet confirmed that there were no fractures and all was fine. We were to give Bella a pill over each of the next three days, and after paying a bill of 100 euros, we left.

Four days later we returned to the surgery as instructed for a check up. By then Bella was much better, she still had a slight limp, but was much improved.

As soon as we entered the treatment room, the woman vet immediately declared that Bella would need an operation. We were puzzled as the X-rays had shown no signs of a problem and the first vet had confirmed this. "Oh, we get this problem with small dogs like her," she huffed, tapping on her computer keyboard, and ignored our comments about it happening twice each year.

Bella was given a rather more thorough examination by a second vet and he nodded in agreement. We were then asked to see the traumatologist. When he arrived, Bella was given more prods and pokes and he confidently confirmed the diagnosis of the other two vets.

We stood in white-faced silence as the woman vet continued to tap enthusiastically on her keyboard, whilst making that sharp sucking in of breath sound that I do so detest - it always means trouble. We then entered the fantasy and frightening world of surgery - complete with anaesthetics, drugs, treatment and recovery times.

"Did we also want specialist heart and blood tests before the operation?" the vet barked. We were told that this was essential in case Bella was not fit enough and would die during the operation. "That will be 800 euros, but you can pay over three months", she smiled, handing us the detailed printed estimate.

"Oh, and by the way, she will also need the second leg doing as well, so shall we call it 1600 euros for the two?"

As a parting shot, we were then told that it was important for Bella to take a special, and expensive, pill lasting two weeks until the time of her operation. Each pill cost 13 euros - we bought one and drove home in silence. We both felt uneasy because what we had just heard just was not convincing and contradicted the findings of the first vet.

Two weeks later, Bella has just come back from her usual boisterous run on the field. Her leg is now fully recovered and, no, we did not give her that expensive pill nor will she be having the operations. It is now clear to us that the surgery saw us as pet-loving Brits ready to hand over 1600 euros, at the expense of Bella's well being.

Just as with human health, alternatives, therapies and drugs should always be considered before surgery. In Bella's case, the diagnosis for unnecessary surgery would have led to great expense, and treatment that would have caused her unnecessary pain and distress for several months.

Needless to say, I am concerned at this attempted exploitation of our love for Bella. We are now seeking a vet who can give sufficient professionalism, morality and decency to the care and welfare of our pets before attempting to exploit us and our furry friends.

Vets at home

Recently, there have been worrying reports in the medical journals commenting upon the revelation that visits to doctors' surgeries and hospitals increase the populations' blood pressure. No real surprises there I guess. After all, who really does enjoy a visit to the doctor?

It is the same with dogs and cats visiting the vet. All animals feel considerable stress when moved to unfamiliar surroundings, meeting unfamiliar people and smelling unfamiliar smells. Yet, we bundle Pedro and Maria into the car for their annual jabs and wonder why many dogs and cats freak out in the vet's surgery.

I was dreading Bella's and Mac's annual visit to the surgery this week. First of all we have disengaged ourselves completely from the previous surgery where, because we are 'Expats in Spain' and considered by some as ripe for exploitation, the vet and her cronies had decided that Bella needed an unnecessary operation designed to extract 1600 euros from our pockets.

Fortunately, we discovered in time that this was a scam and Bella's pulled muscle healed naturally in a couple of weeks without operations or medication. However, it severely shook our confidence in a veterinary practice that we previously had confidence in, although it could have been cleaner and less chaotic.

A number of friends recommended their vets and we visited several. However, I was still uneasy about taking our cat and dog to one, unless it was an absolute emergency. Bella, for example, detests women vets in particular and, on the last occasion, it took four adults to pin our small dog down for a routine examination.

The distress that the event caused Bella and ourselves just cannot be right and we resolved at that time to go to a vet who had some basic understanding of animal psychology. Similarly, was it right to bundle our cat into a holdall, place him in a warm car for 30 minutes to wait in a crowded surgery with unfamiliar sounds and smells? There must be a better way.

It turned out that there was - in the shape of a mobile veterinary surgery. A mobile surgery arrived outside our door and the friendly and knowledgeable vet proudly gave us a tour of his mobile surgery.

It was a converted ambulance, complete with an onboard operating theatre, equipment for blood tests, oxygen supply and all manner of equipment. It was at least as well equipped as our previous vet's surgery, as well as being much cleaner and better organised as a bonus!

The vet collected his bag, several instruments and the necessary drugs and administered them to Bella and Mac on our kitchen table. Both animals appeared to be happy and relaxed, even after insertion of the required microchip for Mac.

Bella adored the new vet, and particularly after she had received several treats from his well-stocked bag. He spent time talking to both animals, as well as giving us advice about heartworm and other issues. Was it expensive? No, the price was less than the cost of a visit to our previous vet.

I am not saying that this is an answer in all situations, and in an emergency it may be quicker to travel to the nearest veterinary surgery. However, for non-essential treatment, a mobile veterinary surgery seems to be the much better option.

How to do it

Debit Cards for Expats

Many of us have fallen out with credit cards. Individually, as well as nationally and globally, we can now see that being encouraged to spend beyond our means has been a bad thing. One early catch phrase during the launch of the credit card revolution was that "Access (remember those?) takes the waiting out of wanting," which now seems rather hollow, as we now realise that our 'wanting' costs considerably more, if left unpaid on the credit card.

Many people have also experienced considerable worry and illness due to increasing personal debt, particularly at a time of severe recession and job losses.

Debit cards are a useful alternative. A direct charge against our bank account helps to remove immediate temptation, and encourages us to spend within our means. However, personally, I am reluctant to use these cards online or with traders that I do not know, because of potential fraud.

Now that I live overseas, I rely a great deal on purchases on the Internet; indeed eBay has been a real lifeline for items that I cannot purchase at a fair price on the island. I prefer to keep my bank debit card for cash withdrawals, and not run the risk of my card being used by some overseas scam operation to clear out my bank account. So without credit or debit cards, what are the alternatives?

Well, you could ask your bank to set up a second current account with a debit card, just for Internet transactions. However, this usually means additional charges for running the account, as well as charges for the issue of the card, which can be very expensive in Spain.

Some Spanish banks issue prepaid cards specifically for use on the Internet; although useful, I have found that they are expensive and one that I tried involved a visit to the bank to top up, as this feature was not available online. Such an arrangement is not ideal if you suddenly find a good value flight online, and need to complete the transaction quickly.

I now use prepaid debit cards issued in the UK. One that I use is issued free of charge, and the other card costs around ten pounds for three years. I can transfer money instantly from my main UK bank account into the prepaid card. These funds are then converted into euros (or dollars if you prefer) and are instantly available for use.

They can be used to withdraw cash from most cash dispensers worldwide, at a cost of 1.50 euros for each withdrawal (maximum 300 euros) or used for purchases in any establishment that accepts debit or credit cards in the usual way.

There are no additional charges for operating the account, which is a bonus. The only downside appears to be that you have to have a UK address, but this can usually easily be overcome. (See an earlier 'Letter from the Atlantic', "What's your address?")

One of the companies that I use, FairFX, offers a particularly good rate of exchange - far better than at airports, of course, or even the Post Office. I can view the transactions online, top up from my mobile phone, as well as operating a second card for my partner.

Best of all, it is a secure way to do business online, and it is reassuring that, should the worst happen, I would only lose the top up amount on my card, which I deliberately keep at a low limit and top up only when needed.

Prepaid debit cards are also a good idea if expats have children living in the UK, or maybe attending university. They can be given a card linked to the main account and then their card can be topped up as and when they need, or deserve, some additional cash! It is ideal for Christmas and birthday presents too!

There are now a multitude of such cards available, but, as an expat, only a few meet my criteria of being either free or cheap to run, offer a good exchange rate, online access and choice of currency. I have a card that I operate in euros only in Spain and the Canary Islands, one in dollars for purchases from, and when visiting, the US, as well as one in sterling for UK purchases and visits.

I hope this information helps. Further information about the cards mentioned is available on the Expat Survival section of my website. If you come across some better deals that are suitable for expats, do please let me know and I will share the information with other readers.

Complaining in Spain

One of the worst things that the newly arrived expat quickly faces is the sudden inability to complain if things go wrong. Spain may well be a member of the EU family, but when it comes to complaining, the expat would be wise to remember that it is a very different culture and pace of life. After all, isn't that why we left the UK in the first place?

Forget shouting, being abusive and banging your fist on the table, because, at best, you will be completely ignored or possibly sent to the end of the queue to sulk, or, at worst, you may see the inside of a prison cell for a few hours.

One of my first experiences of trying to make a complaint in Spain was about our new home in the Costa Blanca. We had no water and the electricity was on builder's supply, which meant that it was very erratic.

Most of our neighbours had similar problems, and after endless weeks of waiting, breakdown of electrical appliances, unfulfilled promises and several freezer loads of food destroyed, we had enough.

At that time I had very little Spanish to help me, other than the ability to order a bottle of wine and basic food items. Staff in the builder's office could speak English; after all we had bought a property from them in English a few weeks earlier.

However, when it came to after sales it was strictly Spanish speaking only. Out of desperation one morning we went to the sales office to complain, and it was a true eye opener.

We joined the queue of angry people. Two harassed young women were trying to do their best to calm angry clients. It was a painfully slow process and involved many telephone calls, long, tedious explanations and much sharp sucking in of breath - a mannerism which I detest at the best of times, because it usually means that there is no likelihood of anything being done - ever.

After about half an hour in the queue we noticed one unshaven man in a grubby vest and an unpleasant disposition, who had arrived in the office before ourselves; he was clearly very angry and could hardly contain himself.

When he reached the counter, the young woman smiled and asked what she could do to help. His response was to bang on the table and shout considerable abuse at the poor woman. Although we were angry too, I found myself feeling very sorry for her having to deal with this thug of a man.

He snarled and growled about his problems, which I gather was something to do with a faulty water heater. The young woman watched and said nothing as she pressed the buzzer beneath the desk. After what seemed like several minutes of abuse, two police officers burst into the office, pistols bristling at their side and duly handcuffed this protesting lump of foul-mouthed humanity.

We all cheered as our countryman was bundled into the waiting police car outside. It was several days before we saw him again, greatly subdued. I believe that he became a much better person after his night in the cell.

In contrast, other neighbours took a very different approach. An attempt at speaking Spanish in a calm manner, together with the occasional box of chocolates worked wonders. I also recall these neighbours taking the office staff for a meal on one occasion!

As a result, our wise neighbours were connected to the mains water and electricity supply very quickly, as well as having many of their other problems attended to promptly and courteously. We very quickly realised which was the most successful approach when complaining to the builders.

Customer service in Spain is good overall, but you have to be patient, polite, prepared to give up a full morning and persevere. The golden rule is to remain calm and cheerful, despite the surging feeling of anger inside.

Remember too that whoever is trying to help you also have their own problems and issues to deal with, and they will get around to dealing with your problem eventually. Yes, basic good manners and an attempt at the language go a long way in Spain, as it does in most other countries.

Paternity leave

The UK's deputy Prime Minister, Nick Clegg, recently announced government proposals for revising the paternity leave arrangements for new dads. This proposal could see dads getting up to ten months paid leave after their babies are born, by allowing parents to divide the existing year's maternity leave between them.

Unless you actually run a small business, I can see a lot of merit in these proposals, and it should help our youngsters to get off to a better start in their young lives, as well as helping to ease the stress of having a new baby in the home for both mum and dad.

Babies are the hope and future of any society and, as a teacher, there were few things more exciting for me than to help and watch very young children grow and develop in confidence, gain knowledge and understanding and an awareness of other people and their environment. After all, whether we have our own children or not, all children are the hopes and dreams of our futures.

Over the years, these values have been recognised and supported in most civilised societies, who have felt that a collective investment in children is an investment in society as a whole. Sadly, as we have seen with the increase in tuition fees in the UK and the erosion of the principles of 'free education for all', these values appear to be under threat or, depending upon the colour of your politics, are requiring "readjustment to meet changing fiscal needs."

'Baby Bonds' and grants that used to be given to newly born babies in both the UK and Spain have been withdrawn in both countries in recent months in response to the global recession.

Although some may not need these grants, it was an indicator of the value and hope that we place upon all children, and symbolic of a collective hope and determination that all children should have a good start in life.

However, all is not lost. The Canarian government has announced economic assistance for parents expecting more than one child, which can financially break a family. Parents will be given up to €1,200 for each child per year until the children are 10 years old.

The actual amount given will depend upon the number of children born and the family's earnings. Maybe both new schemes do not answer all the need, but at least it is better than nothing, and continues to recognise the value of children to society.

So what has all this to do with the new arrangements for paternity leave in the UK? Contrast these recent developments to the birth of babies in the Canary Islands just a few generations ago.

After the birth, mum would be expected to resume work and normal household duties right away, whilst dad took to the matrimonial bed for a few days 'to recover from the birth' and to receive relatives, friends and neighbours who were no doubt anxious to meet the new baby.

This local custom was seen as an important step for dad to bond with the newly born baby, as well as a social occasion to welcome the new child into the world and was, no doubt, an excuse, for quite a few toasts, and whilst mum was scrubbing the floor, no doubt. Somehow I don't think modern dads would get away with this kind of behaviour nowadays, even if it is called 'paternity leave'!

What's your address?

As soon as the initial euphoria and exhaustion of a move to another country has evaporated, many expats quickly discover that they also need to have an address in the UK. Even if, at first sight, with a new home and address in a newly adopted country it no longer seems necessary, most expats quickly find that a UK address is almost essential.

Many UK expats will, for instance, continue to quote their old UK home address to banks, credit card companies, driving licence authority etc., even though it is not strictly legal. In my experience, financial institutions in particular, often became rather nervous when told of my impending escape to a country in the sun; for example, would they mind sending on policy renewal forms and replacement bank cards to my home in the Canary Islands?

Sometimes, the response to such a request was met either with a curt reply that smacked ever so slightly of jealousy, or as if I had decided to move somewhere off the planet. "Oh no, Sir, we have no procedures for sending post overseas. We will have to close your account", or "Please do not tell me that, it may cause problems with your licence, insurance policy...", have both been responses that I have received to such a relatively simple request.

After all, we are still talking about Europe and not a move off Planet Earth aren't we?

When it comes to ordering items from the Internet or mail order catalogues, you will be met with much the same response. Notable exceptions are Amazon - both UK and USA, who are terrific, as well as QVC who will take a 'foreign address' in their stride. Similarly, with eBay orders; some traders will send overseas and others will not.

I won a beautiful camera at a knock down price recently on an eBay auction, only to be informed by the seller that he did not ship overseas. The Orkneys were somehow most acceptable, but not the Canary Islands. Had he heard of registered post overseas, I mused?

If you are fortunate to own or rent a home in the UK, maybe a relative or helpful neighbour would be willing send on your post from time to time? Expats that I know often quote their son's or daughter's address, or that of a close friend or neighbour, but, over time, this well-meaning arrangement often ceases to be efficient, and important post can be left unattended for many weeks.

Teething babies, flu and appalling weather, making a trip to the Post Office impossible, are some of the more likely excuses, although I did hear of one case recently where a newly arrived puppy chewed up, and was sick on, three months of bank and credit card statements for one unfortunate expat. Be warned, there are other ways!

Personally, I use a UK mailing service. I have tried several such companies over the years, and most have been very good, but the one that I currently use is excellent. It gives me a UK street address, sends me an email or text message whenever a letter or parcel arrives at their office.

I then log on to their very clever online system, and tell them if the item should be sent on to my home in the Canary Islands, stored, opened and scanned (which saves postage costs) or shredded. This company will send mail to anywhere in the world and makes ordering items online very simple. I can see a photo of the envelope online and can easily determine if it is yet another promotional leaflet to be shredded, or something important that I should ask to be forwarded.

This service is not particularly cheap, but it is reliable and blisteringly efficient and gives me peace of mind. With this service under your belt, expats can focus on what they do best - relaxing, and enjoying the sun!

I also use a similar service in the USA that allows me to order electronic goods at particularly good prices, which can then to be forwarded to my home. Again, this is not a cheap service, but some goods can be purchased at particularly advantageous prices and sent on, whilst still making a substantial saving.

For more information about these services, have a look at my website, under the section 'Expat Survival'. I hope these suggestions help.

Learning the Language

I am often asked what I see as the main priority when planning to move abroad. In my experience, planning to be an expat doesn't work quite like that; it is more often a spontaneous reaction to events, maybe a new job or a response to sudden ill health or maybe an unexpected windfall.

Learning the language and remaining open-minded to the culture that you find yourself in, is my usual answer. Even a basic knowledge of the fundamentals of the language will make life much easier in a newly adopted country. If nothing else, it is usually appreciated by the locals, who realise that you are making an effort and, in my experience, most will go out of their way to help you.

I well remember a small, but vociferous group of expats in Spain, endlessly demanding that Town Halls, police stations, doctors' surgeries, hospitals etc. should offer a free translation service for expats. They resented paying the 50 euros or so fee that private interpreters charged. I used to point out that if such services were offered in English, why not also in German, Russian, French, Norwegian and all the other languages represented in the country?

You could imagine the outcry from taxpayers in the UK if such a service was demanded by the multitude of nationalities now represented in the UK. In my view, the responsibility remains firmly with the expat to make an effort and, in doing so, enriching their own experiences and culture of their newly adopted country.

It is easier said than done, I hear several readers muttering. Yes, I agree, and as someone who has never found learning languages easy, I tend to dismiss the view that languages can be taught to anyone of any age.

Maybe, with an effective teacher, one-to-one tuition and plenty of time for regular lessons, good progress can be made. However, the reality for most expats is that they are either working too hard to make time for lessons, or are not working and do not have enough spare cash to pay for them!

When I arrived in Spain, I knew very little Spanish. I enrolled for one of the free Spanish classes for expats offered by the Town Hall. The intention was good, but when I arrived for my first lesson I realised that the lesson would be with one teacher and forty students at all levels of ability for only 45 minutes a week. This was hardly the stuff for effective learning, and could do far more harm than good.

I tried one of the popular courses on CD. It was very well constructed, but very boring. I lacked motivation and quickly gave that up. Meanwhile, my partner, who had to learn Spanish quickly in order to get a job, enrolled on a four-week intensive Spanish course at a local language school. It was for two hours a day, five days a week for a month.

This approach was on a one-to-one basis with a well-qualified and experienced teacher, and with plenty of homework. The lessons were very expensive, but it was highly effective.

I was fortunate to find a local teacher with whom I had twice-weekly lessons. This arrangement worked well until I moved to the Canary Islands. However, I was able to continue my lessons twice a week for one hour by using the Internet and Skype.

The teacher was still in the Costa Blanca, but was flexible in his approach and this meant that I could arrange the lessons around my own busy schedule. These lessons worked very well for me, because they were mainly conversational, about real issues that interested, as well as motivated, me.

In addition, I accepted a language course that was offered free-of-charge by the Canarian Government. This course was a computer-based distance-learning course for English speaking expats, and monitored by a tutor who also gave feedback and assessments.

I was very pleased to achieve the diploma offered after just a few months. The course also had the advantage of adding a firm vocabulary and grammatical structure to what I had already learned from other methods.

I have learned to take my language learning less seriously than in the early days. I used to worry that my mistakes could cause great offence to the listener; I have had a few of these experiences!

However, I no longer worry if I make a mistake. I do the best that I can with what I know, wave my hands around a lot and speak clearly; I am also very good at mime. Usually, the recipient of my antics understands me and knows that I am making an effort.

The only exceptions that I make are in cases relating to legal, financial or medical issues, which have potentially serious implications, and when I would also take along someone confident in the language.

I am told that the best way of learning a new language is take on a lover who speaks the language of your choice. However, that can cause some problems, but whichever method of learning you choose, just enjoy it!

"You need new track rod ends, Sir"

This seemingly endless refrain used to greet me whenever I collected my Mini from an MOT service station in the UK. No, my Mini was not one of those lovely BMW look-a-likes, but a genuine Mini - just as its creator Alec Issigonis had intended, and by all accounts complete with poor track rod ends, even though it was not a particularly old vehicle.

If it wasn't track rod ends, it would be new brake pads, suspension, bearings or sub frame. I am not talking only about my Mini, but a whole range of vehicles over the years that I was driving in the UK.

A failed MOT meant that often owners were unable to drive their vehicle away from the garage, as the car was deemed unroadworthy; and was therefore held as captive for the garage to do whatever it wished to both the car and owner's wallet. It was a classic open cheque book scenario, and one where I and many others were left with the distinct feeling that we were being 'ripped off'.

In later years, I would have my annual service and pre MOT check just before the official test was due, but I rarely survived the MOT inspection unscathed. Like so many UK consumers, I would challenge the bill, eventually pay up and look for another garage to use in the future.

Of course, there were some good garage experiences too, but on reflection I have to say that these were rare.

Moving to Spain and the Canary Islands was a breath of fresh air, in more ways than one. Over here we have a system of government inspections of vehicles. The tests are called ITV tests (Inspección Técnica de Vehículos), which take place at approved centres.

These centres are not garages, but a network of testing stations approved by the state to focus solely on vehicle inspections. The centres can be easily located by going to the website of the Dirección General de Tráfico. An appointment may be made in person, by telephone or on line.

The owner of the car is present when the vehicle is tested and, indeed, takes part in the testing process, such as applying brakes and switching on headlights when required. This process can be a little disconcerting the first time a non Spanish speaker takes part, but the staff are usually helpful enough and it is easy to get by with a mixture of Spanish and English, together with quite a lot of arm waving.

The vehicle's registration document (permiso de circulación), technical papers (ficha technico) and proof of valid motor insurance must be taken to the testing centre and shown when the vehicle is tested.

The test is thorough. The vehicle is placed over a pit, on rollers; it is prodded and shaken, seat belts are tested, lights are switched on and off, tyres are checked, exhaust emissions tested and recorded, and brakes and shock absorbers checked for efficiency.

Cars are also checked for the condition of the bodywork and mirrors, windscreen and wipers. During my last ITV, the vehicle in the neighbouring test lane to mine was failed, because the passenger door would not open and this was rightly considered to be a safety violation.

When the tests are complete, a document is issued detailing any faults found (Infracciones Graves & Infracciones Leves). Any fault listed in the section Infracciones Graves (serious fault) must be repaired before an ITV can be issued.

If a vehicle fails the test, the owner is given a document listing the faults. The repairs must be completed within two months of the test. However, if the repaired vehicle is returned to the ITV centre within 15 days, the owner will normally receive a discount on the cost of the repeat test.

Should the car not be retested during the two-month period, notification will be sent to the Jefatura Provincial de Tráfico, and the car may be deregistered.

The inspection process is usually completed in about 20 minutes when, if successful, a new sticker will be stuck to the windscreen to prove that the car has been inspected together with a reminder when the next test is due. The process is relatively cheap, efficient and effective.

New cars are first tested after four years and must be inspected and tested every two years thereafter until the age of 10. Any car over 10 years of age must be tested annually.

More information about the ITV testing process, and requirements for cars, motorcycles and caravans are available on the Expat Survival section of my website.

No process is ever perfect and I am sure that some readers will have had negative experiences. However, my experiences have been pleasant ones; I know that my car has been checked thoroughly, as I have been part of the process, and do not feel that a 'get rich quick' garage is exploiting me.

Complaining

"I just wanna be OK, be OK, be OK..."

Our move to Spain and the Canary Islands has not been without some stress. However, few things have given me as many problems, anger and, very occasionally, amusement as my endless dealings with that big beast of a telephone company, Telefonica. Love 'em or hate 'em, I dare say that very few of us have escaped their clutches.

My first encounter with 'The Big Beast' came shortly after moving into a new housing development in the Costa Blanca. Obtaining a reliable electricity and water supply were both considerable challenges, but none more so than getting a telephone. I recall standing in endless queues with other equally frustrated expats of all nationalities, and sometimes the shop closing before anyone was available to attend to our needs.

I have witnessed grown men cry with anger and frustration at the sheer incompetence of trying to get a telephone line installed. I joined the waiting list for connections, only to be told one year later that my name had been removed from the list. This apparently was the procedure if a connection is not available within six months! Sadly, no one had thought to tell us of this ruling. We managed to get a connection just before we left the area.

As a reporter, I quickly became aware that I could supply an entire week's submissions based purely on horror stories about 'The Big Beast'.

I remember visiting one terminally ill lady with a heart condition who was unable to leave her home. Her husband had tried in vain for months to get a telephone installed. The mobile signal was poor in their area and it was essential that the couple had a form of communication for an emergency, as well as a modem link for a new form of electronic gadgetry linked directly to the hospital.

When I visited the couple, I enquired if there were technical reasons as to why they could not be connected. The couple shook their heads and pointed to the telephone junction box just a few metres from their home.

Now living in the Canary Islands, I continue to face similar incompetence and unreliability. Rarely a month goes by without some kind of problem rearing its ugly head. I find that I become even more irritated by the endless rendition of that inane song, "I just wanna be OK, be OK, be OK..." when I am put on hold for twenty minutes or so.

A few weeks ago after the alarm company reported that my landline was not working, I called 'The Big Beast'. I was given a twenty-minute rendition of "I just wanna be OK, be OK, be OK..." before a very cross-sounding woman advised me that I had been disconnected, because I had not paid my bill two months earlier. As I have had a direct debit set up for a number of years, I was puzzled. The conversation with the señorita ended abruptly when she enquired if I would like their television service added to my account. Somehow I thought not.

Eventually, after several days of calls and complaints, and a reconnection charge of 25 euros, the line was eventually reconnected. Enquiries with my bank revealed that a direct debit was set up and there were sufficient funds available to pay it, yet the debit had not been presented.

I was also told that the company had changed their trading name during the month in question, and there were many customers in the same position as myself. However, even after filing a formal complaint, my claim for a refund of the reconnection charge was denied.

Last month the line failed again. I was told that there was nothing that they could do for 48 hours, but would I like to consider having their new television service added to my account? Er, presumably I would need a working telephone line? However, a few days later an engineer appeared and agreed that the line was not working.

He disappeared, only to reappear a few minutes later, having driven to the telephone exchange, to announce that the line had been disconnected in error, as there was some confusion about whether we had an ADSL connection with Telefonica or not. Wisely, we did not! The line miraculously started working again.

Two weeks ago, the connection failed again. I called "I just wanna be OK, be OK, be OK..." and was told, "There are technical problems in your area. Can I interest you in...?" she began.

Six days later the line started working again. There was no prior warning, no reason given, no apology and no refund of line charge.

As I write this, I am happy to report that we have finally broken free from 'The Big Beast'. My mobile phone contract with the same company has finally ended, we have ADSL with another company, and we have just transferred our line away from "The Big Beast".

I'm not saying that my telecommunications life will be problem free, but at least I no longer have to listen to that inane rendition of "I just wanna be OK, be OK, be OK..." I really am OK now, thank you.

A Tortoise called 'Aduana'

Despite all the positive aspects of living in the Canary Islands there are, as in all things in life, a few negatives too. One of my main irritations is the Aduana (Customs) process. Even though the Canary Islands are part of Spain, and within the European Union, we are outside of both for the purposes of taxation.

This state of affairs is of great benefit to residents and visitors alike, who can buy all the luxury goods they can afford whilst on holiday, and pay only 7% IGIC (local tax) instead of IVA or VAT in Spain of 21% and in the UK at 20%. However, there are downsides too.

If, for example, I wish to purchase an item from outside the Canary Islands, I invariably end up paying both the tax from the country of origin, as well as the local Canary Islands tax, plus a delivery surcharge of around 15 euros!

Fortunately, those very good people at Amazon have now seen the error of their ways after I challenged them recently. I was surprised and delighted to receive a hefty refund for all the VAT that I had paid on items delivered to the Canary Islands over the last few years. Yes, if you contact them after delivery they will refund your VAT!

Now back to the Aduana. This organisation does seem to move at the pace of a tortoise on Prozac. They appear to be totally unaware that we have a global economy nowadays and that many of us also like to shop globally. After all, there are some things that cannot be purchased in the Canary Islands.

Take, for example, Amazon's very clever new device - the Kindle eReader. I do confess to having some interest in the success of this product as I have several publications in this format. However, if you live in Spain and the Canary Islands, the only realistic option, until recently, was to purchase the Kindle from Amazon.com in the US.

On the face of it, this was not a problem. Ordering from Amazon.com is quick and simple, apart from having to deposit an additional sum for local tax to be paid to the Aduana upon arrival. The tracking information was fascinating; my Kindle left Kentucky in the US and arrived in Germany the following day. The package arrived in Madrid the next day and was in Las Palmas the day after that.

I think that four days for a package to get from the US to the Canary Islands is rather good. However, my box of goodies sat in the office of the Aduana in Las Palmas awaiting release for around seven days, and without any attempt to contact me.

Some time ago, my publishers in the UK sent me a box containing copies of my latest book, 'Letters from the Atlantic'. One month later I was still waiting for the box to arrive when I received a telephone call. The publishers had just received the box of books back in their offices, undelivered.

Undaunted, they tried again. Three weeks later, the same thing happened and the box was returned to them. No reason given, and was just returned. "We send all over the world, even Oman despite the recent troubles, and the books always get there. It is always the Canary Islands that are the problem," commented one irritated member of staff.

The whole episode was just a little embarrassing. I had been receiving messages from friends, family, readers and the media in the UK commenting and asking me about my new book, without having actually seen a copy myself. Out of desperation, I ordered a couple of books from Amazon - they were delivered five days later. Now, I am not suggesting that all this is the fault of the Aduana, but I do have my suspicions!

How big is your gnome?

I have to confess that I am not a great lover of gnomes. No, I don't mean the 'real' ones that appear in fairytales, but the depraved garden variety. Toadstools, seagulls, fairies and wishing wells I can accept quite happily, but the grinning garden gnome, wearing that totally impractical, ostentatious and irritating red hat really makes me see red (if you excuse the pun).

A garden is meant to be a thing of beauty, an extension and reflection of our own personalities; so why is it that some people fill their gardens with these malevolent, desperate looking creatures?

Many people think that garden gnomes are quite innocent, sitting quietly with their fishing rods dunked into a sea of concrete that will never catch any fish. Do they really think that they are sitting on a toadstool for their benefit?

No, they are planning their next attempt to undermine the human race. Besides, most gnomes are far too plump and well fed for any self-respecting toadstool to survive under their weight.

I am not quite sure why I react in this way. Maybe it was some horrific tale that I read in childhood - after all, some fairy tales actually are not at all fit for children (the authors are not called the Brothers Grimm for nothing!).

Maybe they remind me of a much-detested Sunday School teacher from my early years or, as I have long suspected, the uncanny likeness between them and the much disliked Great Uncle Gilbert.

I used to think that gnomes were a 'Brit thing' and I recall many quite attractive gardens in the UK ruined by rows of these miserable creations. I recall another uncle who had dozens of things, which he brought into the garage each winter and spent his spare time repainting them ready for the next season.

As a child, I always had the desperate urge to pull the communication cord on a fast moving train. Similarly, I also had the desire to blow the heads off as many of these evil creatures that I could find in Uncle's garage. No, don't worry, I never did either, but I wish I had.

I thought I was safe in Spain, and maybe more so in the Canary Islands. Don't believe a word of it. Today, I walked past a neighbour's house - they are a nice old couple who spend a lot of time developing their small garden.

It has moved on from being a stony desert left by the builders into a thing of beauty, a delight on the eye and full of colour for most of the year. Neither is there a prickly cactus in sight, which is remarkable - given where we live.

As I walked my dog Bella past the garden gate, we stopped as usual to peer inside at the latest development. Horror upon horrors! As I peered over the gate, the gaze of another being met my eye.

The evil gaze that met me was from the largest and most malevolent looking creation that I have seen for some time. It was the tallest, plumpest gnome that I have ever seen! He grinned and, I thought, winked at me. Bella growled menacingly and I walked smartly on. Bella seemed relieved to get away too.

So there we have it. Our early nightmares come back to haunt us in later life, it seems, wherever we are. Mine lives just a few doors away and is a constant reminder of the nightmares of childhood.

We also have other neighbours, well known artists, who have a passion for drawing, painting and designing naked gnomes. The first time I saw them I was rather taken aback, but at least they had hung up those silly red hats.

As with humans, it is rather hard to look intimidating without wearing a shred of clothing. Apparently the pictures sell rather well in a specialist market and I was given a free sample, but that is a story for another time.

The Sunshine Expat

One thing that amuses, intrigues and sometimes irritates me as an expat in Spain has been a small, but vocal, group of expats who have been fortunate enough to escape to the sunshine, yet spend their time complaining about life back in the UK. The 'sunshine expats', as I call them, sit on their sun drenched terraces, gin and tonic in hand, philosophising on what they see as the failure of Britain to somehow justify their move, and good fortune, to another country.

The Government, Health Service, state of the roads, young people, the weather, Nick Clegg, Jeremy Clarkson, and the economy are all likely targets for ridicule. "Britain is dead," or "We had to get away because of the weather" or "There is no future for anyone in the UK" are all comments to be heard on many expat balconies and British bars, and particularly during those first heady months of an escape from Britain.

Is it really an escape? It is interesting to note that many of these expats, who are so keen to criticise the country of their birth, still wish to maintain their UK voting rights, driving licence, UK address, dentist or doctor (if they can get away with it), even though they no longer visit the UK and have no real experience or understanding of current issues.

On a sadder note, it is interesting to see how many of these 'sunshine expats' quickly desert their adopted country as soon as they hit trouble and return to the UK. Unemployment, relationship break-up, illness and bereavement are all deciding factors in a decision to "return home". It is understandable, of course; during times of great stress we need to be with our families, friends, in a country whose systems we can understand and have the fluency in language to deal with the things that frighten or worry us.

Recently, I have been reading some of the comments and questions on several expat blog sites, which are often best avoided if you wish to keep your blood pressure down. Many of the current questions and comments currently relate to money held in Spanish banks.

Questions are usually along the lines of "Is it safe to keep my money in a Spanish bank?" "Should I transfer my money back to a UK bank?" or "Should I move my savings to an off shore account?" An urban myth is creeping into expat bar chat that, should the worst happen and the euro collapses, investors in Jersey or the Isle of Man would somehow be at less risk than if they had left their savings in a Spanish bank account. As for transferring funds back to the UK, just remember Northern Rock!

Such advice tends to overlook the fact that security guarantees for deposits in Spanish banks are similar to those offered by UK banks. If all such government guarantees fail, then a few quid in Jersey is hardly likely to make any difference as we will all be heading for the lifeboats!

Meanwhile, quite a few offshore banks and investment brokers are making a tidy profit by encouraging expat panic and the transfer of funds to offshore bank accounts, so be warned!

For me, and many others like me, being an expat is all about taking the rough with the smooth, and I am not about to bail out as soon as the going gets tough. Learning more about the culture, making an effort with the language, getting to know local people and customs is what being an expat is all about.

It is one of life's real adventures and, taken in the right spirit, can be a life changing and wonderful experience, as many have already discovered. Yes, sunshine and cheap booze is a bonus, but it is not the only reason to move and, for many expats that I know, life in their newly adopted country is where it feels right to be, it is from personal choice and not just the result of an accident of birth.

Expat Life

Beware of Submarines and Drug-smuggling Grannies

I am not sure why, but a recent news item from Columbia set my mind racing about submarines. The story was all about Colombian soldiers seizing a fully submersible drug-smuggling submarine capable of reaching the coast of Mexico, and reminded me of how determined and devious drug smugglers can be.

The story is even more astonishing because previous drug-carrying vessels found in Colombia were only semi-submersible, with part of the structure always remaining above the surface. However, the submarine recently discovered could operate completely underwater, and was estimated that it could hold eight tons of drugs.

Apparently, the submarine could submerge up to three metres deep and was equipped with a five-metre periscope and had the ability to travel to the coast of Mexico without surfacing, a journey taking eight to nine days.

It was a heavy investment for the drug smugglers, as the submarine had taken six to eight months to build at a cost of about 1,500,000 euros. Colombia has seized at least 32 semi-submersible vessels designed to smuggle drugs over the years, including a dozen last year.

All this puts into context the number of pensioners who have been caught smuggling drugs from the Canary Islands in recent months.

Apparently, drug smugglers prefer to recruit elderly and disabled people to carry out their drug running operations, because no one would suspect an elderly, innocent-looking granny of carrying drugs in her bra, or that smart looking elderly gentleman of carrying a supply in his colostomy bag! Maybe a submarine is the next logical step for the determined smuggler?

Talking of submarines, the recent Wikileaks revelations suggest that the US Government approached the Spanish Government via their embassy in Madrid with the suggestion that Las Palmas could be developed as a useful port for the American fleet, and with a view to an increased US presence in Africa.

In addition, it seems that there were also suggestions that the current military cooperation agreement was adjusted to include Las Palmas on the list of ports authorised to host nuclear submarines. Understandably perhaps, the Spanish government has refused to comment on such revelations.

Can you imagine nuclear subs ducking and diving off our islands? Well, maybe they do already. Finally, if you do enjoy deep sea diving or scuba diving, just be very careful where you put your flippers!

The weather influences walking

Sometimes, if I am in the right mood, I get a rather warped pleasure from reading recent research papers. I know that researchers will have worked long and hard over many months, if not years, to complete their work, and many of these research papers are extremely valuable.

However, some are just plain silly, are totally irrelevant and, in my opinion, do not justify a research grant.

Some of the worst offenders are published and often misinterpreted in the tabloids as space-fillers and can be highly amusing, particularly if they will make good headline grabbers such as "Eating fried cockroaches adds ten years to your life!"

A recent study by researchers from one university in the US examining obesity has just come to the enlightening conclusion that climate affects our walking habits. Indeed, people will walk more if the weather is right. No argument with this so far.

Researchers observed pedestrians in nine cities around the world - Santa Cruz in the Canary Islands; Kilmarnock and Glasgow in Scotland; Rousse in Bulgaria; Gliwice in Poland; Oulu and Jakobstad in Finland; Sion in Switzerland; and Ithaca in the United States over 170 days from late autumn (I refuse to use that ghastly Americanism, 'fall') to early summer.

Living in the Canary Islands, I am not too keen of walking when the temperature is over 40°C, nor is my dog, Bella. Mindful of government health advice, as well as words from Noel Coward's "Mad dogs and Englishmen go out in the noonday sun", I tend to walk for a short distance when it is hot and walk for longer distances when it is cool, or preferably in an air conditioned shopping centre.

Similarly, would you really set foot outdoors for pleasure if you happened to live in Glasgow or Kilmarnock? I think not. How about a nice stroll outside during winter in Finland? I suspect you would need an ice pick to prise your mouth open.

The researchers came to the staggering conclusion that a 5-degree temperature increase led to a 14 per cent increase in pedestrians on the streets and a shift from snow to dry conditions was associated with an increase of 23 per cent in pedestrian traffic. Now, would you believe that people actually like walking when their feet are allowed to move?

"Now, let's ban snow and the cold weather and heat our pavement areas. Forget global warming, let's just get them walking," I can hear the Mayor of London booming to the policymakers at City Hall.

The authors concluded that more people would walk if town planners would design neighbourhoods that counter extremes of temperature and use surfaces that help people to walk.

Prompt removal of snow and efficient drainage would also encourage people to walk. How about council staff out on the pavements with shovels, salt and grit early in the morning? Didn't they used to do that when Grandad was a boy? What a good idea!

The study concluded with the insightful comment about how people will walk more if they are prepared for the weather. Hmm, given the recent debate in the UK about the relevance and quality of degree courses currently offered by UK universities, with poor old media studies and computer games degree courses being considered as "irrelevant", I recommend the 'Walking in the right weather' course as an ideal candidate for the budgetary chop.

Mowing the lawn

So, what exactly is the point of grass? One of the household jobs that I used to hate in the UK was the weekly chore of cutting the grass. It was a job that seemed to last all Saturday morning, if the weather was decent enough, and I seemed to spend most of my time trying to get the mower to work and collecting up the grass clippings afterwards.

Edging the lawn, removing moss, clover and daisies seemed such an unnecessary and time-consuming chore. Worse still, two days after I had cut the grass the job really needed doing again.

Then came the blissful luxury of patio tiles! Creating a tiled patio area around our homes in the Costa Blanca, and later in the Canary Islands, seemed such a sensible idea with no more cutting of grass ever again!

Once the design has been chosen, the site levelled and the tiles firmly stuck down on the cement that would be that - forever! Hmm, red rain? Surely that would be an easy matter to sort out with a hosepipe? Sadly this was not the case.

I have watched neighbours struggle and become obsessed with the after effects of red rain in the Costa Blanca. At first it was rather amusing to watch the frenetic activity on neighbours' patios after a rainstorm.

Patio furniture, tiles, steps, banisters and balustrades all had to be carefully washed and scrubbed within minutes of the rain stopping. After all, this red dust from the Sahara was pretty powerful stuff and it seemed to get into places, cracks and crevices that you would not think possible.

Then of one our neighbours discovered the idea of using Agua Fuerte - an acid that when diluted with water would bring back the showroom shine to the newly laid tiles. What a find that was! Word soon got around the neighbourhood and we were all soon busily washing down our patio tiles with a solution of this potentially dangerous mix.

Here in the Canary Islands we have just finished washing our patio after a heavy storm. Fortunately it was not of the red rain variety, but after weeks without rain it has certainly brought with it a fair amount of dust and dirt.

Grass is a rare sight in this part of the Canary Islands. I read in one of the trade journals recently that artificial grass is a growth export business with hundreds of rolls of the stuff being sent to the Canary Islands from the UK and Germany.

Indeed, we realised just a few months ago that our dog, Bella, had never seen grass, let alone chased a ball or rolled on it as our dogs in the UK used to. For a treat we drove her to a park some distance from our home and watched her cavort, roll and play in this green paradise with the greatest of pleasure.

Sadly, she also peed with excitement several times and so my sincere apologies go to the Town Hall for the brown patches that no doubt appeared on this carefully manicured lawn a few days later.

Sitting on my patio chair enjoying the last of the day's sunshine with a glass of wine, I hear the familiar sound of a lawnmower. It is from the neighbours who live just behind our property. They have a small patch of grass, which is about the size of a large tablecloth.

This little patch of Britain is carefully nurtured, watered, fed, fertilised and regularly cut with tremendous pride and the greatest pleasure. They even use a rotary lawnmower to cut the grass when a large pair of kitchen scissors would be more than adequate and the event is over in seconds. I breathe in the faint smell of newly mown grass and my mind goes flooding back to those years of battling with a lawn mower in our Dorset garden.

Do I miss it? Well, maybe I do feel a little nostalgic.

The Lollipop People

I do apologise if you thought you were about to read something about people selling ice cream products. No, instead I am talking about the gallant men and women who see our children safely across the roads each day in schools all over the UK.

The correct term is School Crossing Patrol and most are kindly souls, often retired, who are happy to give up a couple of hours each weekday to help children to cross busy roads safely, in return for a small salary cheque at the end of the month. I am sure that we all remember many happy lollipop people from our childhood, films and in picture books.

However, the reality is very different. As a busy head teacher, I have to confess that Lollipop Persons (in reality most were women of a certain age, but I guess I have to be politically correct) were, in reality, the bane of my life.

Along with caretakers, cleaners and lunchtime persons (more commonly known as Dinner Ladies), they often filled my day far more than dealing with curriculum issues, discipline, teachers and children, as well as actually teaching from time to time.

I would sometimes receive calls at 7.00am to tell me that one of my 'Lollipops' had a chiropodist appointment, in-growing toenail or broken false teeth that needed immediate attention.

Consequently, 8.30am would often see me clad in startling luminescent overalls, usually in the pouring rain, ushering the little darlings and their parents across a busy road.

The task was not a pleasant one, because in addition to trying to avoid the children and myself being spread liberally all over the road, many parents would tackle me as they crossed, determined to question me about the latest homework policy decision, a problem with their class teacher and did I know that we had head-lice in the school again?

As the traffic roared past, I was only comforted by the thought that after little Gary had finally stopped picking his nose and decided to cross the road, I had precisely three minutes to dash back to school, park the lollipop, change, grab a cup of coffee and be prepared to take school assembly - no doubt kicking off with "All things bright and beautiful' sung through clenched teeth. How I hated the Lollipop role!

So why was I doing the job, you may ask? Well, in short, no one else wanted to do it. How I dreaded the latest resignation or retirement of the present incumbent. It usually meant weeks of advertising, interviews, police checks and training followed by two days on the job and a determined knock on my door.

"I really don't think the job is for me..." the conversation would begin. This inevitably led to me being back to square one.

"Anyone living and breathing out there who is desperate for a job?" I felt like announcing in the next 'Jobs Vacant' page in the local newspaper.

How envious I am of schools in the Canary Islands. They actually have a real police officer, complete with gun at the ready, to guide children safely across the road. Do vehicles stop and take notice? Of course they do.

Do parents stop them and chat about homework, curriculum and the school disco? Of course not. Over here one does not argue with the police and busy head teachers can get on with the real job.

The Collapse of the Euro?

Spotting a new, repackaged bank account being offered in Spain earlier this week reminded me of an unhealthy trend that was very familiar in the UK a few years ago, and now appears to be arriving here.

"The imminent collapse of the Euro! The Euro is about to implode, but that doesn't mean you can't make a profit" screamed the advertisement on one web page that I spotted today.

"The collapse of the Spanish housing market is good news for many! Make sure you profit!" was the good news announced on another site. Good news for whom exactly? Certainly not, the young Spanish couple who can no longer afford the mortgage and whose home has been repossessed by the bank, or the middle aged British couple who have been forced to sell their dream home in the sun for a song, because both have lost their jobs and they no longer have an income. Good news for some indeed.

Rest assured, I am not about to develop an argument in support of the euro: disaster may strike, but then again it may not. Remember the scare story a few years ago that a great chunk of rock on the Canary Island of La Palma was about to fall into the sea and create a tsunami that would destroy most of the east coast of the USA?

Urban myth would suggest that this was a scare story invented by some of the US insurance companies, to 'encourage' householders to take out or increase their insurance cover.

Whether or not an insurance policy would really be of help in such a national emergency is open to debate; the tsunami may or may not occur in the next few million years or so when, I guess, most of us will no longer be concerned anyway.

As far as I am concerned the only real certainty, other than death and taxation, is that most financial advisers and banks look after themselves, and hang the consequences for the general public. Why is it that so many speculators, investment companies, financial advisers and traders are salivating at the very thought of the "imminent collapse of the euro"?

There is a quick profit to be made, of course. Indeed, there are a number of examples of very wealthy individuals and corporations that have made substantial sums of money from similar currency collapses of the past.

I have always objected to the 1980s and 1990s phenomenon, when banks and insurance companies began to launch 'financial products'. For me, the definition of a product is something that has been created or made, not merely a repackaging of an existing financial service.

A newly crafted chair, a shiny new car, a new novel or MP3 track are products that have been created by someone, or manufactured for sale.

One example is the ordinary current bank account, which has now been 'repackaged' with membership to a motoring organisation, together with a free electric pop up toaster, into an exciting new 'product', heavily promoted by slick advertising, for which the grateful customer now pays £15 per month.

Is this really a 'product'? Who pays? Well, we all know the answer to that one. For me, the trend of "new financial products" was the beginning of the 'easy talk' about financial services, easy money to be made and making a fast buck, and the debt that individuals, companies and much of the world fell into, and for which we are all now paying the price.

Who remembers endowment mortgages? I recall being told by 'financial advisers', and I use the term loosely, that this would be the answer to our mortgage, and that 25 years later, our home would be fully paid off and there would a rather handsome lump sum to go with it.

Like so many others, I took their advice and took out policies with two companies, such as Equitable Life and Standard Life, which later collapsed, despite both being heartily endorsed by Which? Magazine (The Consumers' Association) at the time.

In short, endowment policies made a lot of money for the 'financial advisers', banks and the insurance companies, but the rest of us were told to "seek compensation".

Fortunately for me, it was early in the life of the policies and was not a critical situation, but I do wonder what happened to those who were nearing retirement when the news of their failed investments broke.

When it comes to money, one thing that I have learned, is that should you make a handsome profit from an investment, it has usually come at the expense of another poor soul, who has been less wise and less cautious.

After all, isn't that what capitalism is all about? So, back to those advertisements, I suggest that expats give them a very wide berth and enjoy a round of golf, or take the dog for a walk, instead.

Maybe I want to go home?

No doors or windows!

The World recession has claimed the hopes and dreams of many expats, as well as local people. Many expats who finally achieved their dreams of a new life and home in the sun have packed their bags and the few belongings that they have managed to salvage and returned to their home countries.

Many cases that I know of have been little short of tragic, although there are some that have left me wondering whether the intending expat should ever have been allowed to leave their home country in the first place!

James and Charlotte moved into their new home full of the usual excitement and hopes for the future. Both had good jobs and hoped to shortly start a family. As with so many, they overstretched themselves and their mortgaged home required two incomes to pay the hefty mortgage bill, credit card bills and new car, as well as the usual day-to-day living expenses.

The couple were already deeply in debt before the young woman lost her job followed by her partner a few weeks later. Unless you are very fortunate, most banks in Spain are not tolerant of mortgage arrears and, rather quicker than in the UK, owner occupiers are soon forced out of their homes and the property is repossessed by the bank, and resold at a knock down price or, more likely in these difficult times, auctioned for a song.

The young couple were given notice to leave, but before they left, they decided it was 'pay back' time for the bank and they decided to take with them whatever they could salvage.

They removed kitchen units, cupboards, and the bathroom suite and shower cubicle. This was followed by removal of the wooden staircase, all windows and doors and metal railings from the front of the house. One thing that did astound me was that they also took all the external patio tiles, as well as indoor floor tiles!

Anyone who has tried to remove tiles will know that it is backbreaking work and it is, in my experience, almost impossible to remove tiles without breaking them. One can only imagine the heartache, bitterness and anger that lay behind these actions.

Another young couple, Grant and Sue, wrote to tell me of their difficult situation. Grant and Sue had lived in their new home for a couple of years, but when both lost their jobs they could not pay their mortgage.

The bank was unsympathetic to their plight, and so they decided to rent out their property and move away from the area to live with friends until better times came, when they could move back into their home.

Grant talked about their problem in a bar one night when he was drowning his sorrows, and soon found a Spanish couple that agreed to rent their home for six months or so. It seemed like an answer to his prayers, or was it?

Foolishly, Grant made the mistake of revealing that unless the rent was paid then they could not pay the mortgage and the bank would repossess the property.

The Spanish couple moved into their home and, being well aware of the law, failed to pay any rent at all. The house was duly repossessed by the bank, the Spanish couple were allowed to remain in the property, as they were now sitting tenants and had a child attending the village school; a situation that provides tenants with additional rights.

Grant and Sue's home was then sold to the sitting tenants for a very low price, and Grant and Sue were left with nothing. Indeed, they still owe a considerable sum of money to the bank, as not all the debt was repaid.

Renting is a strategy that many expats consider if they cannot sell their property and still have to pay the mortgage. However, this can be fraught with difficulties and may lead to heavy fines being imposed if the property is not registered correctly as a property for rent with the Town Hall.

My best advice is to avoid doing this at all costs unless you are absolutely clear about the law in your adopted country. If you should go down this route, you need a good local lawyer and a well-established lettings agency to support and advise you.

Lightning Strike

It is a safe bet that few people living in the UK and Northern Europe will have little sympathy for poor weather conditions in the Canary Islands. At the time of writing we see people facing horrendous weather conditions in the UK with reports of temperatures plummeting to minus 20°C in parts of Scotland, and little better in most parts of the UK.

Daily lives and routines are all thrown into chaos, and the health and safety of the young and elderly in particular are put at risk by the excessive cold, as well as very dangerous road conditions.

As I sit on my sun lounger tolerating a slightly cooler than normal temperature of around 23°C I admit that we have very little to complain about. However, a few days ago many of us witnessed one of the worst electrical storms on these islands for many years.

The islands' government had announced a rare 'Red Alert' warning several days earlier. Schools and many public buildings were closed in readiness for the torrential storms that were heading towards the Canary Islands from the Atlantic Ocean.

After being flooded, within two days of moving into our new home several years ago, we quickly learned the hard way of the necessity of fitting external shutters to windows, as well as attempting to fit thresholds to the bottom of door frames, which are virtually non-existent over here.

I had always taken door thresholds for granted in the UK, but this simple addition to door frames in Spain and the Canary Islands would make such a difference during heavy rainstorms. Without them, water will pour into any room with an external door during rainstorms, and particularly when accompanied by heavy winds.

I started the day with a throbbing headache - a rare, but always a reliable, telltale sign of a heavy storm to come. Dark, black and threatening clouds appeared over the mountains, the town fell silent and even the dogs stopped barking in anticipation of what was to come.

The sound of rumbling and flashes of lightning began, as the rain and wind started and we reached the safety of our home before the torrent that would later turn into a flood.

At three o'clock in the morning we awoke to the most horrendous thunder that I have ever heard. The house shook as lightning shot across the sky, lighting it up rather like it does with fireworks on fiesta days, but this was not to be from the joy of fireworks.

Rain beat down and the wind blew violently against the closed shutters and doors with a mighty force that seemed not to be of this world. I tried in vain to switch on a light, but the power had failed.

As we take a break from cleaning the patios and repairing some of the damage, we hear that at one period during the night, the islands were at the receiving end of more than 7000 lightning strikes and that between 5.00am and 10.00am there were another 8249 flashes of lightning.

At around 6.00am, 1539 negative rays were recorded - these are the ones that go from earth to the sky. I would just like to know which obsessive soul sat and counted them all!

The sun is shining again; the sea is calm, children are on their way to school and the dogs are barking. Lives are quickly returning to normal. The first of the flights from frozen Europe are heading towards Las Palmas airport, full of mostly pasty white and hopeful passengers longing for a week in the sunshine and an escape from worry and all the talk of recession back home. They will not be disappointed.

Apart from some ground water, muddy roads and some clearing up to do, it is difficult to reconcile this calm, everyday scene with the nightmare of the previous night.

Too much of a good thing...?

"Ooo, lovely! 45 degrees in the shade!" exclaimed our friend, vigorously tapping our outside thermometer, as we were desperately trying to keep cool during yet another heat wave. High temperatures such as this are great if you are on holiday, have nothing to do but drink refreshing liquids in the shade of a palm tree, or can sit in an air-conditioned room all day. However, all this can get a bit much for normal day-to-day activities, if such extreme temperatures continue for too long.

Admittedly, these high temperatures are unusual in the Canary Islands, and often only last for a few days as the hot winds are blown from the Sahara. Yet the excessive heat is often uncomfortable for many, not only because the heat disturbs sleep, but also for the associated eye irritations and infections that my ophthalmic surgeon tells me often accompany the hot winds.

Don't misunderstand me, I am not suffering from the usual Brit disease of endlessly complaining about the weather; I left that little bundle of misery back in the UK many years ago, but merely pointing out that adjustments to extreme temperatures do take getting used to.

It has been a strange year on an island that rarely sees such wide variations in temperature. A few months ago, temperatures on the island plunged to around 10 degrees, which some of our elderly neighbours told me was the coldest for 30 years, yet a few days ago temperatures were in excess of 45 degrees, and higher in parts of the south of the island.

During spells of high temperatures, medical alerts are issued by the islands' government and, unlike some holidaymakers who attempt to go trekking during periods of excessive heat, often with disastrous consequences, most people attempt to follow the Canarian way of doing things.

Such changes in day-to-day living include getting up early to complete necessary physical activities and household chores before it gets too hot, having a siesta during the hottest part of the day (a sensible idea at any time of the year anyway), not taking the dog for a walk during the heat of the day, drinking lots of fluids (not alcohol!), as well as shopping in one of the many air conditioned shopping centres late into the evening.

Visitors to the island often ask me about our energy bills and are envious when I tell them that we have no central heating, other than switching on a fan heater occasionally during the coldest parts of the year, or maybe the negligible expense of lighting a few candles on a really chilly evening, remembering that it is all relative to what you are normally used to.

However, the flip side of the coin does mean that many homes on the island now have air conditioning units installed, and these are now used much more frequently now than in previous years, when they were a rare sight in all but the most expensive properties. These units are expensive to run, and mean that what is not spent on heating during the winter months tends to be spent on air conditioning during the summer; so we do not escape high energy bills completely. Island living means that many of us spend most of our time outdoors.

Other than periods of very low or excessively high temperatures, we tend to eat breakfast, lunch and dinner outdoors and, again, with just a few candles for company, which also helps to reduce overall energy consumption.

"What about lack of water?" is another question that would be expats and visitors often anxiously ask. Despite the lack of regular rainfall, sometimes occurring only for a few days in February in the south of the island, I have not known a time when we cannot use hosepipes to wash our cars, hose our patios or to water the plants in the garden.

Underground reservoirs, as well as occasional rainfall in the mountain areas, together with an endless supply of water from the desalination plants, means that this is rarely an issue. After all, we are surrounded by the stuff. As for washing the car? No, it is far too hot for that. I'm off for a siesta!

Hypertension in the Canary Islands

"You are living in the Canary Islands now. You cannot be stressed; it is impossible. No one is stressed over here!" I recall one doctor declaring confidently to the weeping young woman in his surgery one morning. Actually, it was quite clear that this poor woman was suffering from postnatal depression and that she had reached one of the lowest points of her life.

Well, I have news for this doctor, who maybe should undergo a period of retraining, there are many stressed people living in the Canary Islands, just as there are in most other parts of the world. A glorious climate cannot compensate for all the ills of the world and are, no doubt, made more acute by high unemployment, repossession of family homes and relationship breakdowns.

In the last few days, I have seen a friend lose his job, his relationship collapse, as well as having his home repossessed. Each one of these events is, in itself, a trauma of such magnitude and achieves the highest rating on the stress factor tables.

Having all three events happen in one week is potentially disastrous for the individuals concerned and not surprisingly results in an acute level of stress and often much worse. My friend went to the doctor, had his blood pressure taken and, surprise, surprise, was diagnosed with hypertension. As a result he is now on a considerable quantity of medication, which I suspect he will be on for many years to come.

Few people would argue that this individual needed help and support and that, in the short term, medication is part of the urgent help required at a time of crisis. However, there are many people who visit their doctors with relatively minor conditions and return home clutching a prescription for drugs to ease their hypertension, which they do not need.

Recent news from the National Institute for Clinical Excellence (NICE) in the UK revealing concerns about blood pressure tests taken in doctors' surgeries were inaccurate, leading to misdiagnosis of high blood pressure, has confirmed what has long been suspected by many. After all, who enjoys visiting the doctor's surgery or hospital?

For most people it is a period of deep anxiety, not surprisingly leading to a natural rise in blood pressure. Wise doctors recognise this and make allowances, and possibly arrange for a retest. However, this is still likely to be an inflated reading and usually results in increased profits for the drug companies.

I knew one sincere young woman when I lived in the UK who worked briefly as a salesperson for one of the major drug companies. It was her job to persuade doctors to prescribe a certain brand of drug.

The disturbing news was that the orders for supplies of certain drugs came with the carrot of a new laptop computer, 'study trips' to Switzerland and the Bahamas, as well as many other luxury items.

Clearly, it was in a minority of unscrupulous doctors' interest to prescribe and keep patients on these drugs for as long as possible with drugs to deal with hypertension and cholesterol at the top of the list. My friend quickly decided that the job was immoral and resigned.

According NICE, this misdiagnosis of blood pressure has led to as many as 25 per cent of patients being treated for hypertension, who should not have been treated with these expensive drugs. The report has concluded that new technology should be used to confirm a diagnosis of high blood pressure by using a device that measures a person's blood pressure throughout the day.

The new system has been evaluated as being more accurate and better value-for-money when compared to blood pressure readings taken in the surgery by harassed doctors and nurses.

All this sounds like a common-sense policy that, no doubt, the drug companies will hate and hard-pressed governments trying to balance health budgets will applaud. However, I doubt this will really help my friend. What he really needs is a steady job, a stable home and to be reunited with his family.

Embalming anyone?

The unexpected phone call from the mortuary in Las Palmas immediately took my attention. Was I in a position to pay the outstanding account at the mortuary? This really was not the kind of call that anyone would wish to receive first thing in the morning, and particularly when one is struggling to make sense of the world before coffee.

I assured the very pleasant lady at the other end of the line that I had no previous knowledge of their service and that, no, I did not have any kind of account with them, nor did I have one that was due for payment.

However, I assured her, that I would keep her number on file - just in case I needed a spot of embalming in the future. One just never knows when such services might be required. The very nice lady even offered to send me a brochure about their range of services...

The early morning telephone call reminded me of a series of articles that I wrote as a newspaper reporter several years ago about 'Death in Spain'. The series of articles were intended to be a helpful guide in managing one of most traumatic times of our lives, and to assist expats in making the right choices in a country with different customs and traditions in dealing with death.

The articles were not exactly a bundle of laughs and not ones that would, at first sight, encourage advertisers to promote their new restaurant or estate agency on that particular page; however, the series was very popular with readers.

I recall one elderly gentleman who shuffled into the newspaper office to ask for back copies of the newspaper. He was asked why he wanted them. "It's those Death pages", he muttered, "my wife reckons she'll be needing them soon."

Although it is not really a subject that is often discussed over dinner, or over a gin and tonic on the balcony, thoughts about our passing and those of our loved ones should be considered seriously, particularly when living as an expat in another country. Do we have a will in the country that we are residing in, for instance?

I know of many expats who are relying solely on wills made in the UK many years ago. However, lawyers assure me that this arrangement is potentially fraught with difficulties and that all expats should also have a Spanish will, as well as their UK one.

What about bodies? It is traditional, and good sense because of the heat, that bodies are cremated or buried very quickly in Spain, and often within two or three days.

This is in contrast to the UK where bodies can be waiting for two or three weeks before funerals can be arranged. Over here, the final departure is quick, which adds more pressure to be clear about the wishes of the deceased.

In the event of your demise would you prefer to be flown back to the UK at considerable expense, cremated in your newly adopted country and then sent back in a pot, or popped into one of those filing cabinet tomb arrangements that seem to be popular in Spain? What about costs?

Has provision been made to cover the cost of repatriation, for instance? Do you have a funeral expenses insurance policy? These are all very serious issues, I know, but ones that need to be considered carefully and wishes made clear to dependents.

Now, back to that early morning telephone call. I am still wondering why that very nice lady at the mortuary called me.

There is further information on the 'Expat Survival' section of my website. If you have additional information to add, do please let me know.

Expats and Recession

It was not that many years ago that Dot and Bert from Wigan, and others like them, managed to achieve their life-long dreams of opening a bar or a small business in the Spanish Costas and the Portuguese Algarve.

They, and many like them, discovered that a pound went a long way in the countries where the peseta and the escudo were king. It was also a time when the equity locked in many British homes was substantial, and could be released to fund a new lifestyle and a new home in the sun.

As well as the silver entrepreneurs, thousands of British pensioners, many nowhere near the UK state pension age, realised that they too could have a healthier and more comfortable life in the sun, either as 'winter birds' enjoying the delights of an all inclusive hotel in Benidorm during the winter months, at a much lower cost than surviving the UK winter, or making a full time commitment with a new life in the country of their choice.

Low fuel and food costs and comfortable pensions meant a huge improvement in the quality of life for many.

How things have changed. Even though the UK Government, exporters and economists welcome the weakening of sterling to correct the UK's trade imbalances, it is not good news for expat pensioners, who have fixed incomes.

Many British expat pensioners are now facing real reductions in the purchasing power of their UK state pensions, with some analysts citing that their average monthly pension income has dropped by over €250 since the start of the global recession, with British pensioners living overseas having lost out on over €13 billion of their income since the global recession began.

However, the global economic downturn has meant belt tightening for everyone and most expat pensioners are far better off than many Canary Islanders. I know a number of people whose monthly income is less that 600 euros, with many surviving on around 400 euros, which is the subsistence level provided by the Spanish state to those who are entitled to seek help.

I saw an Italian woman on television the other evening complaining, in response to the Italian Government's latest austerity measures, that an income of 1000 euros each month is insufficient to live on. I know many Canary islanders who would be very grateful to receive anywhere near half that amount.

I know times are hard for most people, but a recent Canary Islands' Government survey of more than 500,000 homes surprised and shocked me. The survey shows that around 95,000 households in the Canary Islands survive on an income of less than €350 each month. About 16,000 households survive on much less: just €180 each month.

Complaints about reduced spending power and reductions in the standards of living that we are used to are certainly justified, but it seems that many expats are still in a better position than many locals.

'The Seven Year Itch'

'The Seven Year Itch' is often a term applied to relationships between people that have begun to fail. The early excitement and romance of the first few years of a new relationship have soured, and been replaced by mistrust, disappointment and betrayal.

New responsibilities, work pressures, children and financial difficulties are often the root cause of many problems within a relationship. In many cases, talking over issues, counselling, medical help and realisation that no problem is unique will hopefully avoid leading to the cliff edge and total relationship breakdown. However, in other cases, separation and divorce may be the only answer to such serious problems.

Similar problems also face many expats. In many cases during my time living in Spain and the Canary Islands, I have seen the initial excitement and challenge of a new life in the sun being replaced by anxiety, bitterness and a desire to return to the expat's country of origin at all costs.

Often the drive to return 'home' has been forced upon the expat by an inability to find a new job, or losing a job, financial and relationship pressures and sadly, too often, following a lifestyle that may encourage the increased consumption of alcohol.

Often it is a realisation that living in another country means a disconnection from friends and family in the long term. The unintentional 'out of sight and out of mind' syndrome sets in, with previous good friends and family becoming even more distant.

After all, in time, the expat begins to have little in common with the folks back home.

Living on an island, the situation can become even more acute. The recession and the highest unemployment in Spain have meant that many expats living in the Canary Islands have lost their jobs and, as a consequence, also lost their homes. Regular travel to mainland Europe can be expensive and it is not easy to regularly visit family and friends.

Island living is not for everyone either. The romantic idyll can soon turn into a nightmare of missing certain foods, television, entertainment and, most of all, friends and family.

Even for those who have taken the trouble to learn Spanish, and many do not even make the effort, quickly realise that however long they study or however hard they try, complete mastery of the language will never be enough to share jokes, innuendo and relaxed communication that they enjoy in their native language, unless of course, they manage to find a native partner - and many have!

Seven years appears to be the time that many expats begin to re-evaluate their original decision of making a new life for themselves in the sun.

Rather like a marriage, questions begin to be asked and particularly in the case of those with medical conditions and those reaching old age. It is after seven years or so that I see many expats beginning to pack up and move back to their country of origin.

Hopefully, these expats will realise that nothing in life is ever wasted and it is always better to have tried and failed than not having even made the attempt in the first place.

During my time in Gran Canaria, I have known many people who have enjoyed their time on the island, but reached a point in their lives through work, relationships or finances that they are forced to return to their country of origin.

This can be unsettling for the rest of us, as the expat community is a small one and each departure can make a significant difference. Strangely, I have also noticed that many people who leave the island tend to return a few years later, or certainly have expressed that it is their intention to do so.

These islands are wonderful places to live and returning expats often quickly realise their mistake and make every effort to return once again, older and wiser.

I recall discussing this issue with a visiting psychic several years ago. She listened with interest, retrieved some charts, and pointed out to me that Gran Canaria is at the crossroads of ancient ley lines and, because of this, it is a place of increased spirituality.

This has created the unlikely phenomena that the island draws certain people that it wants to its shores, rejects those it does not want, yet continues to draw back those that leave and the island wishes to retain.

It all sounds like a good plot for a future Doctor Who series. Cynics will, of course, immediately reject this explanation as non-scientific rubbish; however, from what I have observed over the years, I do not easily dismiss the explanation.

The beginning of the end, or the end of the beginning?

The British have always been keen explorers and travellers. A glance through any British secondary school history textbook reveals countless accounts of adventurers and explorers who left the islands that they called home in search of new adventure, new experiences, a new life and, in some cases, a hearty profit. In many ways, the British expat is merely following in the footsteps of these adventurers and explorers.

Maybe it is something to do with living on an island that makes one want to get off it. It could be down to the climate; after all, lack of sunlight, endless rain and cold temperatures can have negative effects upon even the most resilient of people. The rising cost of living and an increasing feeling that our islands are quickly running out of space, also add to the appeal of relocating to another country.

However, I suspect that the real issue has more to do with escaping from an ever increasing frenetic pace of life, and a growing realisation that there is more out there to live for and enjoy.

Being an expat is not always 'a bed of roses', and I hope 'Expat Survival' has gone a little way towards exploding this myth. Living in another country, even the English-speaking ones, brings with it many challenges and frustrations.

These can quickly destroy the dream of living in another country and sharing a different lifestyle. However, the true expat will see these challenges as merely a temporary setback, and sees the bigger picture, and learns from negative experiences.

Some expats do not make it and, after a few years, decide to pack their bags and return "home", wherever that may be. "Home" is a word that I use very loosely and, to me, it usually means the place where my loved ones are, and that, for the present, is the Canary Islands.

I recall asking one expat why he had decided to return home to Manchester. "To be honest, I really do miss the rain beating on the windows when I am warm and cosy inside, and sleeping in a bed with a thick duvet over me," he said, almost apologetically.

You see, it takes all kinds of people and sometimes the things that we miss are trivial yet, over time, grow in importance. For me, I miss friends and family. Not all of them, I might add, and a reasonable distance between some of them is often very helpful!

Over time, I confess to missing things that I had never thought of as important before; for me, such things include daffodils and bluebells in springtime, the smell of newly cut grass, Dorset cream teas and mince pies at Christmas.

I have come to realise that being successful as an expat has something to do with being part of something much bigger, being aware and appreciative of other languages and cultures, learning from people representing other faiths who have something significant to say about life, as well as giving something back when I can.

Over the years, I have come to the conclusion that the least successful expats are those who see expat life as one bathed in endless sunshine and cheap gin and tonics, and where the euro stretches further than the pound did in the UK.

I have met and corresponded with many bitter and resentful expats over the years who continually complain that expat life was not as they thought it would be. Much of it usually boils down to misplaced priorities, sometimes greed and a failure to integrate into a different society.

Many such expats also have one thing in common, the ability to take, but rarely to give. Many have not made the overall 'profit' that they had originally sought, because of wildly fluctuating exchange rates having a negative effect upon their pensions.

They fail to realise that being a successful expat is not about profit, but involves giving something of yourself to your new country, and I do not simply mean in taxation.

I have also met many successful and happy expats who play a significant part in helping local charities and good causes, such as animal rescue, feeding the homeless, visiting prisons, teaching English or comforting the sick and dying.

Many such people give selflessly, without pay or recognition, and it is their way of giving something back.

Although much of 'Expat Survival' relates to Spain and the Canary Islands, there are many common factors relating to expats everywhere, be it in the South of France, Argentina, Canada, South Africa or Australia. Wherever you are, enjoy your new life and remember to give generously of yourself too!

I hope 'Expat Survival' and its companion publications 'Living the Dream' and 'Letters from the Atlantic' will help would-be expats to consider a little more fully what they are letting themselves in for as they "Live their Dream".

www.ingramcontent.com/pod-product-compliance
Lightning Source LLC
LaVergne TN
LVHW021120240125
802072LV00019B/343